Written by Michael Hill

WORLD SUPERBIKE

GIORGIO NADA EDITORE

Giorgio Nada Editore Srl

Editorial Coordinator
Leonardo Acerbi
Art Director
Mirco Lazzari
Foreword
Alan Cathcart
Text
Michael Hill
Italian Version
Carlo Baldi
Graphic Designer
Pol Campmany
Photographs
David Clares
Jairo Diaz
Luca Gambuti
Raffaella Gianolla
Mirco Lazzari

"World Superbike. The 2019-2020 Official Book"
is produced under license of Dorna WSBK Organization
© **2019 Dorna WSBK Organization srl**

©**2019 Giorgio Nada Editore, Vimodrone (MI)**

Giorgio Nada Editore
Via Claudio Treves, 15/17
I – 20090 VIMODRONE – MI
Tel. +39 02 27301126
Fax. +39 02 27301454
E-mail: info@giorgionadaeditore.it
http://www.giorgionadaeditore.it

The catalogue of Giorgio Nada Editore publications is available on request at the above address.

Distributed by:
Giunti Editore Spa
Via Bolognese 165
I – 50139 FIRENZE
www.giunti.it

World Superbike 2019-2020. The Official Book.
ISBN 978-7911-763-0

Press:
D'Auria Printing SPA – Ascoli Piceno (Italy)

INDEX

SBK
MOTUL
FIM SUPERBIKE WORLD CHAMPIONSHIP

Variety is the spice of life, and ever since its very inception back in 1988, the Superbike FIM World Championship aka WorldSBK has been a race series full of contrasts – of men, of circuits, but most of all of machines.

That's been the case ever since the debut WorldSBK round at Donington Park in April 1988, when Davide Tardozzi's four-cylinder in-line Yamaha-engined Bimota won the very first race in the series' history, and Marco Lucchinelli's desmo V-twin Ducati scored victory in the second race later that same day. The battle between twins and fours, with the occasional injection of triples into the technical mix, has been one of the core attributes of the streetbike-derived category for the past three decades.

Which makes it all the more of a watershed moment in the series' history that 2019 was the first ever WorldSBK season which didn't see a single twin-cylinder machine on the grid for any one of the 39 races. That's right – the Ducati desmo V-twin, the single most successful motorcycle in WorldSBK's 32 years of existence, responsible for winning 14

Riders' World titles and 17 Manufacturers' crowns during that time, was completely absent from the race track last season for the first time ever. So in taking Honda's two World titles into account, which it won in 2000 and 2002 after building a better Ducati in the shape of the VTR1000 SP-1/SP-2, this means that the type of bike which has won exactly half of the Riders' World Championships held to date, vanished from the grid practically overnight.

There are several root causes for this, none of which could or maybe even should have been addressed in order to keep the sound of twin-cylinder music in the race programme. Yet that's been a fundamental appeal of World Superbike racing down the decades – the huge variety of contrasting engine notes in the same race that have thrilled race fans, and enticed connoisseurs of mechanical variety to watch and above all listen to road racing's streetbike-derived category.

For the visceral appeal of savouring different exhaust notes is an undeniable element in the thrill we all get from watching and especially listening

to performance motor sport. That's something which MotoGP™ rule makers were right to recognise in ruling out silencers when the four-stroke category was conceived back in 2002 as a replacement for exactly a quarter-century of raucous ring-ding two-strokes, which practically demanded to be silenced as much for health and safety reasons as anything else!

For the first half-decade of MotoGP™ we were treated to a huge variety of sensational sounds, from the unique roar of the V5 Honda RC211V and Proton VR5, to the strident scream of the Aprilia RS Cube, via all sorts of different ways to create a four-cylinder contender, whether the V4 Ducati Desmosedici or Suzuki GSV-R, or the in-line fours of Yamaha and Kawasaki. That glorious orchestra of different sounds pertained until the advent of the 800cc formula in 2007, which ended up resulting in all manufacturers phasing their engine's crankshafts to produce more or less the same engine sounds, irrespective of whether their new motor's format was a V4 or an inline-four. That's a situation which sadly continues to exist today – whereas with production

streetbike-derived racing aka WorldSBK, there isn't the possibility to rephrase the engine internals for better grip or enhanced handling, so what you get in the showroom is what you see on the racetrack!

This has left WorldSBK as the home of mechanical variety – if not perhaps to the same extent as, say, the series' 2001 season. That year, besides the lusty, angry-sounding double-bass aria of the Ducati 996R and Honda VTR1000 SP-1 90-degree V-twins, on which that year's ultimate World Champion Troy Bayliss and defending title-holder Colin Edwards slugged it out for the World crown, fourth-place finisher Troy Corser's 60-degree V-twin Aprilia RSV1000 (on which he won the first two races of the season) had a baritone beat to its narrow-angle motor's exhaust note, while the occasional privateer wildcard riding a V4 Honda RC45 provided the timbre of a tenor. Peter Goddard's three-cylinder Benelli Tornado by contrast sang like a contralto – deep and mellifluous at low rpm, higher-pitched and haunting when he revved it out. And then there were the more gentle-seeming fours from Suzuki, Kawasaki

and Yamaha, each singing like a soprano, and indeed sometimes arguably close to screeching. Well, not every singer sounds like Maria Callas or Kiri Te Kanawa…

Fast forward to today, and despite the loss of the twin-cylinder bikes, WorldSBK racegoers are still regaled with a glorious cacophony of sounds from the current lineup of Superbike contenders. Indeed, three very different-sounding bikes finished in the first three places in the 2019 WorldSBK points table, with winner Jonathan Rea's Kawasaki ZX-10R a good old-fashioned in-line four-cylinder screamer of a bike, of the kind dubbed the UJM/Universal Japanese Motorcycle that Superbike racing was founded to cater for in California in the mid-1970s. Today's BMW and Honda in-line fours manifest the same design strategy. But the Yamaha YZF-R1 on which Alex Lowes wound up third in the 2019 championship is a very different kind of in-line four to the six-time title-winning Kawasaki ZX-10R, with its unique crossplane crank that delivers a flat, gruff exhaust note, in obtaining improved traction and enhanced throttle control, so Yamaha contends.

But in 2019 for the first time ever, multi-World Champion's Ducati came to the grid with something other than a desmo V-twin. Instead, its new-for-2019 Panigale V4-R was an unashamed derivative of its Desmosedici MotoGP™ contender – and in bringing it to the WSBK grid, Ducati re-introduced the meaty drone of a 90-degree V4 to the WorldSBK playlist, for the first time since the demise at the turn of the Millennium of Honda's similar-but-750cc RC45. Championship runner-up Alvaro Bautista rode the wheels off it to score victory in the first eleven races in the championship, before defending champion Jonny Rea began putting him under pressure, with the result that the WorldSBK pendulum swung in the other direction. But Ducati is back as a serious championship contender, and it's going to be well worth watching the Italian brand's newly crowned BSB champion Scott Redding join Chaz Davies in trying to stop Jonny Rea making it six

World titles in a row in 2020. Oh – and listening to him doing so, too, of course!

Alan Cathcart

Hampshire UK – October 31, 2019

SBK «

MOTUL

FIM SUPERBIKE WORLD CHAMPIONSHIP

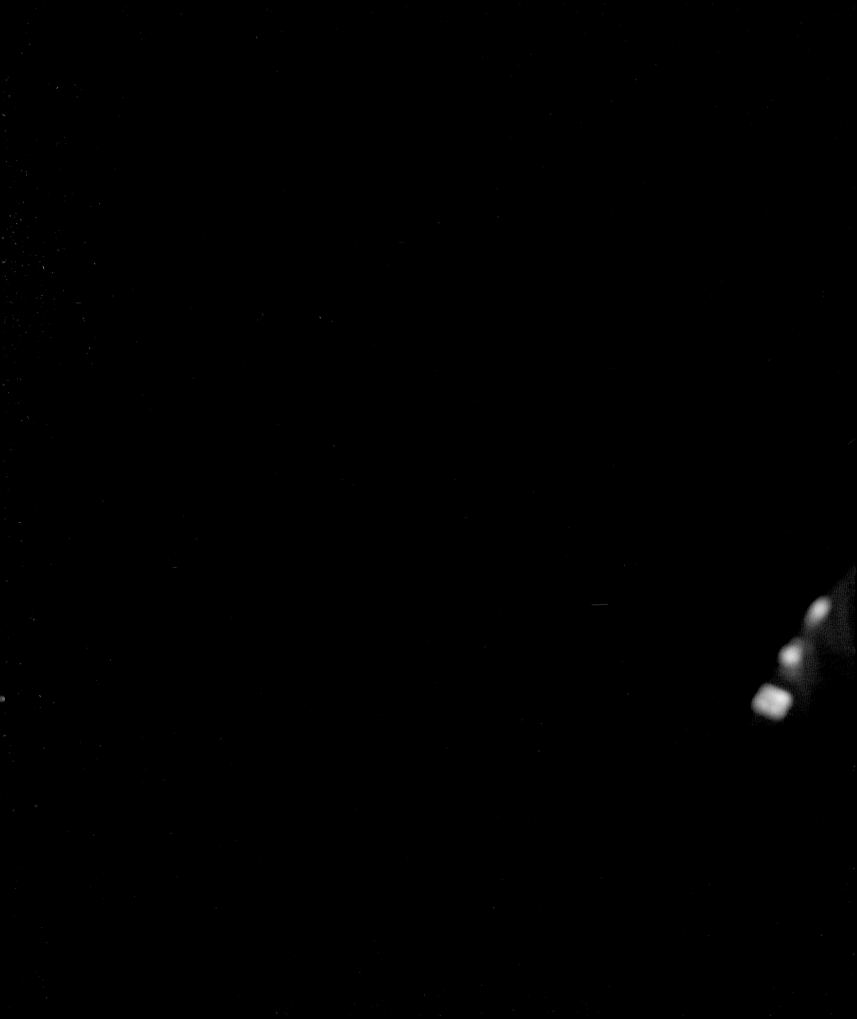

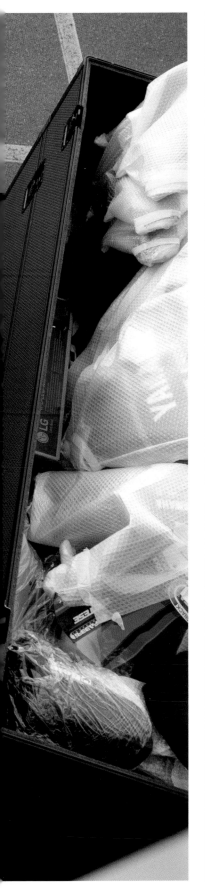

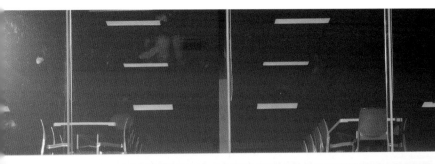

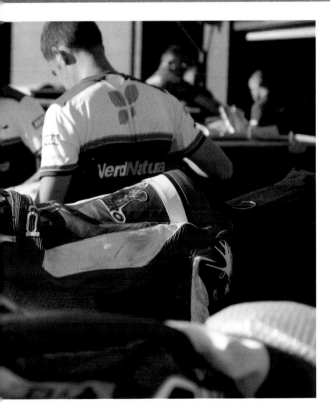

1 VENUES & CLASSES

2019 VENUES

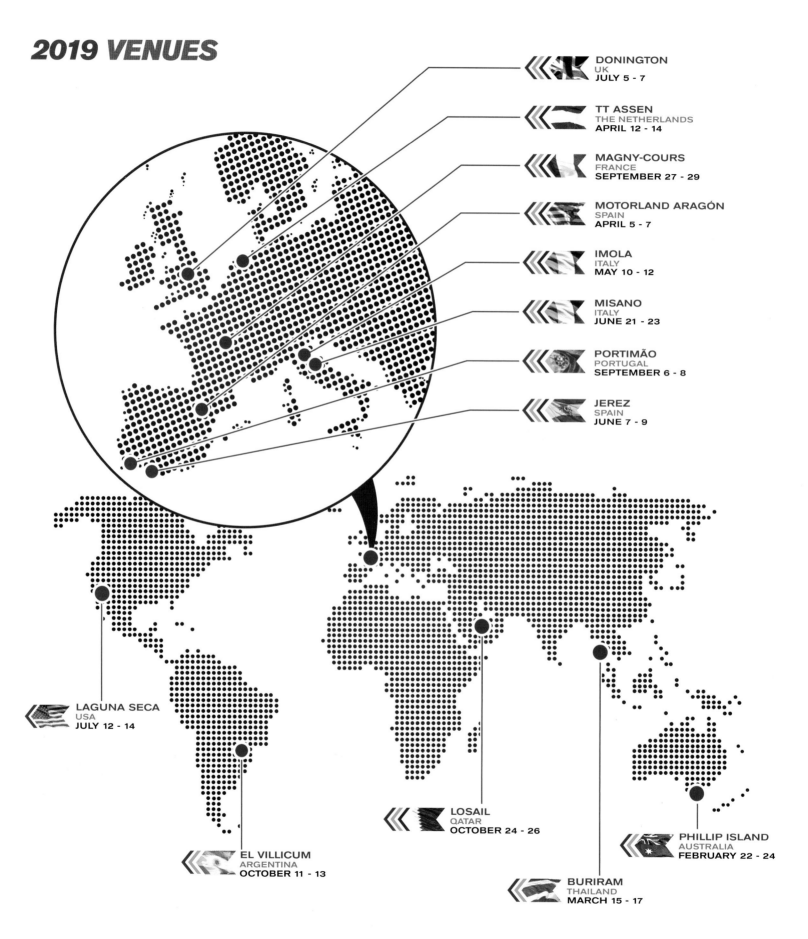

DONINGTON
UK
JULY 5 - 7

TT ASSEN
THE NETHERLANDS
APRIL 12 - 14

MAGNY-COURS
FRANCE
SEPTEMBER 27 - 29

MOTORLAND ARAGÓN
SPAIN
APRIL 5 - 7

IMOLA
ITALY
MAY 10 - 12

MISANO
ITALY
JUNE 21 - 23

PORTIMÃO
PORTUGAL
SEPTEMBER 6 - 8

JEREZ
SPAIN
JUNE 7 - 9

LAGUNA SECA
USA
JULY 12 - 14

EL VILLICUM
ARGENTINA
OCTOBER 11 - 13

LOSAIL
QATAR
OCTOBER 24 - 26

BURIRAM
THAILAND
MARCH 15 - 17

PHILLIP ISLAND
AUSTRALIA
FEBRUARY 22 - 24

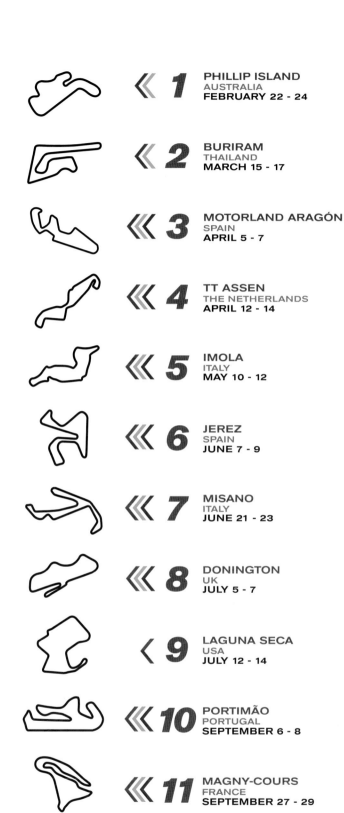

《 1 PHILLIP ISLAND
AUSTRALIA
FEBRUARY 22 - 24

《 2 BURIRAM
THAILAND
MARCH 15 - 17

《 3 MOTORLAND ARAGÓN
SPAIN
APRIL 5 - 7

《 4 TT ASSEN
THE NETHERLANDS
APRIL 12 - 14

《 5 IMOLA
ITALY
MAY 10 - 12

《 6 JEREZ
SPAIN
JUNE 7 - 9

《 7 MISANO
ITALY
JUNE 21 - 23

《 8 DONINGTON
UK
JULY 5 - 7

《 9 LAGUNA SECA
USA
JULY 12 - 14

《 10 PORTIMÃO
PORTUGAL
SEPTEMBER 6 - 8

《 11 MAGNY-COURS
FRANCE
SEPTEMBER 27 - 29

《 12 EL VILLICUM
ARGENTINA
OCTOBER 11 - 13

《 13 LOSAIL
QATAR
OCTOBER 24 - 26

2019 CLASSES

SBK《 MOTUL
FIM SUPERBIKE WORLD CHAMPIONSHIP

Motul FIM Superbike World Championship

Featuring production-based Superbikes from five manufacturers, the Motul FIM Superbike World Championship is the premier class during a typical WorldSBK weekend. Road machines in essence, for racing purposes modifications to exhausts, suspension, brakes and some engine parts are permitted. Three races, one on Saturday and two on Sunday in 2019 meant 39 races would decide the overall World Champion.

SUPERSPORT《
FIM WORLD CHAMPIONSHIP

FIM Supersport World Championship

World Supersport features mid-range production based Supersport machines. The bikes may be smaller and less powerful, but the Supersport class produces some amazing on-track battles and is vitally important to manufacturers too.

SUPERSPORT300《
FIM WORLD CHAMPIONSHIP

FIM Supersport 300 World Championship

Created as a feeder class and introduced in 2017, this production-based series is devoted to building rider potential and discovering new talents worldwide. With a minimum rider entry age of 15, WorldSSP300 expanded massively in 2019 with more than 50 permanent entries taking to the track on their #roadtoWorldSBK.

2 SEASON REVIEW

 *Phillip Island*
22 - 24 February

Bautista blitzes the opposition down under

YAMAHA FINANCE AUSTRALIAN ROUND

Álvaro Bautista made a dream start to his WorldSBK career after storming to three wins from three starts. With the top fifteen covered by little more than a second after Free Practice 2 at the iconic Phillip Island circuit, nobody could have predicted the dominance of the Spaniard when the lights went out in all three races down under.

WorldSBK Race 1

Starting from third on the grid for Race 1, after reigning World Champion Jonathan Rea destroyed the lap record in Tissot Superpole, Bautista wasted no time in hitting the front where he opened up a lead of more than six seconds by quarter race distance. Behind him was typical WorldSBK action with Rea, Haslam and Lowes locked together in the early stages.

Haslam eventually got the better of his new Kawasaki teammate, the former WorldSBK runner-up relishing the chance to once again mix it with the world's best. The 'Pocket Rocket', as he is affectionately known, was looking comfortable in second when he lost the front of his ZX10-RR at Turn 4, allowing Rea to finish the opening race of the season on the podium, albeit 14.983s behind runaway winner Bautista.

Marco Melandri went under the radar as the opening round of 2019 got underway but, as any fan of World Superbike knows, you can never count out the multiple race winner. #33 started slowly but his experience and smooth riding style allowed him to preserve his tyres; the Italian pipping Alex Lowes for the final podium place in his return ride for Yamaha by 0.050s at the flag. Melandri was also the top Independent rider.

Lowes was credited with fourth, two seconds ahead of teammate Michael van der Mark and Toprak Razgatlioglu, who fought his way to sixth after starting fourteenth on the grid.

Tom Sykes was pleased to bring the all-new BMW S 1000 RR home in a solid seventh ahead of Sandro Cortese who had an encouraging WorldSBK debut in eighth. Michael Ruben Rinaldi impressed in ninth on his Phillip Island debut with Chaz

PHILLIP ISLAND CIRCUIT

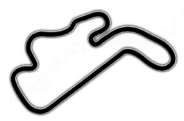

Race 1

1	**Álvaro Bautista**	22 laps
2	**Jonathan Rea**	+14.983s
3	**Marco Melandri**	+16.934s

Tissot Superpole Race

1	**Álvaro Bautista**	10 laps
2	**Jonathan Rea**	+1.176s
3	**Leon Haslam**	+5.072s

Race 2

1	**Álvaro Bautista**	22 laps
2	**Jonathan Rea**	+12.195s
3	**Leon Haslam**	+12.454s

Race

1	**Randy Krummenacher**	16 laps
2	**Jules Cluzel**	+6.157
3	**Federico Caricasulo**	+7.338s

Davies coming home tenth, the 2018 runner-up still finding his feet with the all-new Panigale V4 R. Leon Haslam salvaged the final World Championship point after remounting to finish fifteenth.

Tissot Superpole Race

All eyes were on the lights for the start of the first ever ten-lap Tissot Superpole Race. With all riders aware that tyre choice may play a part, and the fact that the top nine finishers would not only score World Championship points but also form the top nine on the grid for Race 2 later on Sunday, tension was high; it was Jonathan Rea who made the initial running, the four-time Champion more than up for taking the fight to Bautista who once again was in the mix from the off.

Leon Haslam rode sensibly, seemingly content to bag a maiden 2019 podium in third, although the same couldn't be said for Rea who pulled off some audacious moves at the ultra-fast Turn 1. Rea and Bautista passed each other several times a lap as the pace at the front saw the duo repeatedly smash the race lap record. As the race entered the final lap, Bautista, who was now back in front, dug deep to secure his second win in as many races from Rea, who bagged another runner-up spot.

Behind Haslam, Alex Lowes brought his Yamaha home in fourth ahead of Michael van der Mark and Marco Melandri, who lost two places on the final lap, slipping to sixth at the flag.

Sandro Cortese went one better than he had in the opening encounter of the weekend, finishing seventh, with Michael Ruben Rinaldi and Eugene Laverty completing the top nine.

WorldSBK Race 2

After winning Saturday's Race 1 by the largest margin ever in a dry WorldSBK race, Álvaro Bautista was on another planet once again in Race 2, romping to another win, albeit by a slightly smaller margin of 12.195s.

Despite another valiant effort by the duo of KRT Jonathan Rea and Leon Haslam, the all-new Ducati Panigale V4 R was unbeatable at the circuit that the Spanish rider openly declares as one of his favourites.

It may not have been as intense for the win as it had been for the Tissot Superpole Race but the fight between Rea and Haslam had everyone on the edge of their seats, the reigning British Superbike Champion making it clear that he was not back in the series to play a number two role.

Edging away from their rivals, #1 eventually got the better of #91 to make it three second places for four-time Champion Rea and a return to a full-distance race podium for Haslam. Another three-way Yamaha scrup for fourth raged throughout the twenty-two-lap encounter with Michael van der Mark this time getting the better of Alex Lowes and Marco Melandri this time. Melandri once again claimed top Independent honours.

Chaz Davies continued to grow in confidence aboard the second factory Ducati, the #7 finishing seventh after overhauling Sandro Cortese in the final laps.

Eugene Laverty added another top ten finish in ninth, crossing the line just ahead of Leon Camier who gave Honda their first points of 2019. Leandro Mercado just missed out on the top ten but was satisfied after his first weekend aboard his new Kawasaki, whilst top BMW finisher in Race 2 was reigning FIM Superstock 1000 European Champion Markus Reiterberger in twelfth.

Ryuichi Kiyonari finished fifteenth to score his first WorldSBK points since 2009.

WorldSSP

Randy Krummenacher dominated the opening round of WorldSSP, overcoming the additional challenge of a mandatory pit stop to change the rear tyre to win his third career World Supersport race from Jules Cluzel and Federico Caricasulo.

Krummenacher, who celebrated his 29th birthday on race day, was on top of the timing sheets throughout testing and all official practice sessions at Phillip Island. Claiming a front row start for the sixteen-lap encounter, the Swiss rider made a solid start, running just behind early leader Cluzel before taking the lead ahead of his pit stop. Electing to make his compulsory stop on Lap 6, the #21 emerged from Pit Lane a fraction ahead of multiple WorldSSP runner-up Cluzel whose GMT94 squad changed both front and rear tyres.

A mistake from Caricasulo saw him initially set off from outside his pit box with the rear stand still attached to his Yamaha YZF R6 after his tyre change, costing the young Italian valuable seconds and ultimately ruling him out of a race winning challenge.

At the front Krummenacher eased away, eventually taking the win by 6.157s from Cluzel who hung on to second despite a time penalty for a pit stop infringement. Caricasulo recovered to take the final spot on the podium.

Behind the top three a multitude of riders swapped paint, with Spanish rider Héctor Barberá, reunited with the Team Toth squad that saw him mount a title challenge several years ago in the 250cc World Championship, securing the thirteen points for fourth.

Thomas Gradinger edged Hikari Okubo for fifth, with Corentin Perolari finishing seventh on his Phillip Island debut. Peter Sebestyen rode the race of his career to finish eighth ahead of his new teammate Jules Danilo who snatched ninth from Loris Cresson in a photo finish.

There was Aussie delight following Tom Toparis' spirited ride to eleventh and first-time points for Dutch rider Glenn van Straalen who finished thirteenth.

PIRELLI
PIRELLI
MOTUL
MOTUL
MOTUL
MOTUL
Kawasaki
aruba.it
RACING
DUCATI
FIAMM
2
1
ACERBIS
ACERBIS
SBK MOTUL
FIM SUPERBIKE WORLD CHAMPIONSHIP

Chang International Circuit
15 - 17 March

Triple number two in Thailand for #19

Round 2 of the 2019 Motul FIM Superbike World Championship saw the riders take to the track in arguably the hottest conditions ever recorded during a WorldSBK event at the Chang International Circuit. With temperatures close to 40 degrees, it was Álvaro Bautista who romped to pole position, his first in WorldSBK, after an intense Tissot Superpole session saw the top five riders on the grid under the existing lap record and separated by 0.7s.

WorldSBK Race 1

Álvaro Bautista made it four from four after another convincing win in the opening race at the Chang International Circuit. Initially taking the lead, it was Jonathan Rea who came out fighting by overtaking the #19 Ducati several times with a series of hard but fair moves that saw the pair eventually collide at Turn 3, with Bautista lucky to stay aboard. Dropping back into the clutches of a trio of Yamahas, Bautista showed his class, setting three consecutive fastest laps to close back in on Rea. With a new lap record in the bag, the Spanish rider decided that enough was enough, making his move to retake the lead. Once out front he was never headed, taking the win by an impressive 8.217s at the flag as Rea once again finished in second place.

Alex Lowes converted his front row start into his first podium of the year after fending off a late challenge from teammate Michael van der Mark, Leon Haslam and Marco Melandri who was top Independent rider in sixth.

Superbike Rookie Sandro Cortese held off Michael Ruben Rinaldi and Tom Sykes for seventh, whilst Toprak Razgatlioglu came out on top by less than a second in his own private battle with Jordi Torres for tenth.

Chaz Davies tipped off at Turn 3 in the early stages. He remounted to claim the final World Championship point in fifteenth.

Eugene Laverty was lucky to escape serious injury after brake failure saw the #50 have to jump off his Ducati Panigale V4 R on the approach to the final corner on Lap 3. Despite a valiant attempt by his Goeleven squad, who attempted - with the help of the factory Ducati team - to build a second bike, he would take no further part in the weekend.

MOTUL THAI ROUND

Chang
INTERNATIONAL
CIRCUIT

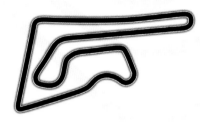

FIM SUPERBIKE WORLD CHAMPIONSHIP

Race 1

1 **Álvaro Bautista** — 20 laps
2 **Jonathan Rea** — +8.217s
3 **Alex Lowes** — +14.155s

Tissot Superpole Race

1 **Álvaro Bautista** — 6 laps
2 **Jonathan Rea** — +2.042s
3 **Alex Lowes** — +2.457s

Race 2

1 **Álvaro Bautista** — 20 laps
2 **Jonathan Rea** — +10.053s
3 **Alex Lowes** — +12.368s

SUPERSPORT
FIM WORLD CHAMPIONSHIP

Race

1 **Jules Cluzel** — 17 laps
2 **Randy Krummenacher** — +0.939s
3 **Federico Caricasulo** — +1.496s

Tissot Superpole Race

A red flag after six laps ensured that Álvaro Bautista's unbeaten record remained intact, the Spanish rider classified the winner of the fifth race of the season by two seconds following a crash involving local rider Thitipong Warokorn and Leon Camier.

Jonathan Rea, who set the fastest lap of the race, took his fifth consecutive second place of the season from Alex Lowes who put in another impressive performance to finish less than half a second behind the four-time Champion.

Former World Supersport Champion Michael van der Mark headed a closely packed group of riders taking fourth from Haslam, Melandri, Cortese, Davies and Razgatlioglu, who took the final point for finishing ninth.

WorldSBK Race 2

There was a feeling of déjà vu after Race 2 in Thailand and another lights-to-flag win for Álvaro Bautista. A gap of more than ten seconds at the flag underlined his supremacy in the opening six races and, whilst it was clear his Ducati had a significant speed advantage, what was also evident was the Spanish rider's talent. Equalling his own Race 1 lap record, the #19 was unstoppable.

You don't win one (let alone four) World Championship titles for nothing and Rea, who was second once more, acknowledged that whilst second was the best he could do, it was better to take twenty points than finish on the floor.

A valiant effort once again from Alex Lowes saw him challenge Rea throughout the 20-lap encounter before losing touch in the closing stages. He would however finish more than five seconds clear of his Yamaha teammate Michael van der Mark, Leon Haslam and Marco Melandri, who finished in the same order for the third race in a row.

Top Independent rider Melandri crossed the line four seconds clear of Sandro Cortese, whose impressive debut Superbike season continued. The German in-turn was more than five seconds clear of Michael Ruben Rinaldi. Toprak Razgatlioglu and Jordi Torres enjoyed another race-long private battle; the pair crossed the line in a photo finish with the Turkish rider getting the nod by 0.068s.

After looking strong, Chaz Davies suffered a technical problem with his Ducati Panigale V4 R, the Welshman's difficult start to the season showing no sign of improving. He wasn't the only one, though, as Tom Sykes suffered a similar fate with his BMW.

WorldSSP

0.089s separated the front row in Tissot Superpole, so it was no surprise that the second round of WorldSSP was an absolute belter.

Pole-man Jules Cluzel, whose favourite circuit is the Thai venue, wasted no time in hitting the front from fellow front row qualifier Federico Caricasulo. Despite also starting from row one, Randy Krummenacher made a shocking start that saw him drop to eighth on the opening lap.

Controlling the pace, Cluzel hardly put a wheel wrong and responded with ease, it seemed, to every challenge made by his young Italian rival. Caricasulo had his hands full, the #64 having to be precise in attacking Cluzel as any mistake would open the door to the chasing pack which was headed by Moto2 stalwart Isaac Viñales; the Spaniard adapting fast to life in World Supersport.

Not panicking and gradually working his way into the mix was Phillip Island winner Randy Krummenacher, who joined the party at the front with a handful of laps remaining. The fastest lap of the race on Lap 13 put the #21 into contention for the podium with a perfectly timed move on his teammate, guaranteeing the Swiss rider the runner-up spot at the flag.

Leading every lap bar one, Cluzel took the win, the seventeenth of his career to jointly lead the WorldSSP standings as the series headed back to Europe. In second, Krummenacher was more than happy with his recovery ride whilst Caricasulo had mixed emotions in third. Viñales showed he could very well be a contender in 2019 after a fighting fourth, whilst both Raffaele De Rosa and Hikari Okubo finished less than five seconds from the winner in fifth and sixth, respectively.

Finishing fifteenth, Maria Herrera scored the first WorldSSP points for a female racer since Paola Cazzola in Assen in 2010.

≪≪≪ *MotorLand Aragón*
5 - 7 April

Álvaro on cloud nine in Aragón

No Spanish rider had ever won at MotorLand Aragón since it joined the WorldSBK calendar in 2011. By the time round three of the 2019 series was over, one rider had, three times. Converting pole to a win was becoming second nature for the #19 Ducati Panigale V4 R of Álvaro Bautista as the paddock arrived in Spain. Jonathan Rea gave himself a mountain to climb after managing only tenth in Tissot Superpole, while reigning FIM Supersport World Champion Sandro Cortese made it Superbike 'rookies' one and two on the grid after shining in Superpole, the first time this had happened since Magny-Cours 2010.

WorldSBK Race 1

After starting from tenth Jonathan Rea carved his way forward from the off, moving into second on Lap 4. Already 4.4s behind Bautista, the four-time Champion was once again unable to take the fight to the Spanish rider; in fact, he spent the rest of the opening race of the weekend fending off a flurry of on-track attacks from Chaz Davies, Alex Lowes and Eugene Laverty.

A spate of exciting overtakes aided Bautista's escape, crossing the line fifteen seconds clear of the chasing pack, with a new lap record and twenty-five points in the bag.
Rea ultimately took the runner-up spot once more ahead of a jubilant Chaz Davies who showed Aragón pace and ensured his top three race finishing record at the Spanish venue continued for another year. Laverty gave it everything, perhaps a little too much, as the #50 crashed out of the podium fight on the final lap at the final chicane.

Alex Lowes finished inside the top four for the fourth time this year, two seconds ahead of Tom Sykes who in-turn was two seconds ahead of Michael van der Mark.
Sandro Cortese carried his one-lap pace into Race 1, taking a hard fought seventh and top Independent honours, the German comfortably ahead of Toprak Razgatlioglu, Leon Haslam and Jordi Torres who rounded out the top ten.

Leon Camier was once again the top Honda home, albeit almost forty seconds behind runaway winner Bautista. The #2 pipped Marco Melandri to eleventh as Michael Ruben Rinaldi, Ryuichi Kiyonari and a remounted Laverty were the final point-scorers, and in fact the only riders to be classified as finishers.

MOTOCARD ARAGÓN ROUND

MOTORLAND
ARAGÓN

SBK MOTUL
FIM SUPERBIKE WORLD CHAMPIONSHIP

Race 1

1	**Álvaro Bautista**	18 laps
2	**Jonathan Rea**	+15.170s
3	**Chaz Davies**	+15.650s

Tissot Superpole Race

1	**Álvaro Bautista**	10 laps
2	**Jonathan Rea**	+5.791s
3	**Alex Lowes**	+5.906s

Race 2

1	**Álvaro Bautista**	18 laps
2	**Jonathan Rea**	+6.867s
3	**Chaz Davies**	+7.127s

SUPERSPORT
FIM WORLD CHAMPIONSHIP

Race

1	**Randy Krummenacher**	16 laps
2	**Raffaele De Rosa**	+0.094s
3	**Federico Caricasulo**	+0.158s

SUPERSPORT300
FIM WORLD CHAMPIONSHIP

1	**Manuel González**	11 laps
2	**Hugo de Cancellis**	+0.058s
3	**Scott Deroue**	+0.494s

Tissot Superpole Race

The question on everyone's lips before lights out for race eight of 2019 was 'Can anyone stop Álvaro Bautista?' The answer in a word was 'No!'. Another perfect lights-to-flag win by almost six seconds cemented the Spanish rider's name as arguably the greatest first-time World Superbike rider of all-time. Eight consecutive wins at the start of a maiden WorldSBK season is a record.

Never headed, the Spanish fans were celebrating a golden age in World Superbike with their new hero while four-time Champion Jonathan Rea was having to contend with another on-track assault from Chaz Davies, who finally looked at home on the Panigale V4 R and Alex Lowes, who was stringing together an impressively fast and consistent run of front-running points finishes.

Ten laps of inch perfect overtakes from the trio saw Rea responding immediately to any challenge made, guaranteeing himself runner-up spot from Lowes who made it three manufacturers in the top three. Unable to quite match his Saturday pace, Davies had to be content with fourth at the flag after being in the fight for second throughout.

Tom Sykes put in another solid ride on the ever-improving BMW S 1000 RR to beat Eugene Laverty (top Independent rider), who was determined to bring his Ducati home in one piece after Saturday's disappointing spill, by just over half-a-second. Leon Haslam, Jordi Torres and Sandro Cortese completed the top nine, adding Championship points to their season's tally and ensuring that they would make up the front three rows of the grid for Race 2 later that afternoon.

WorldSBK Race 2

Despite starting from second on the grid, Jonathan Rea was unable to put a stop to Álvaro Bautista's winning ways despite giving it his all to stay within touching distance. A winning margin of almost seven seconds doesn't tell the whole story. Bautista pulled away at the front at the rate of a second a lap, at one point leading by ten seconds, before slowing the pace to bask in the adoration of the Spanish fans to take a ninth consecutive race win.

Rea was initially overhauled by Chaz Davies who at one point looked like making it a Ducati one-two, before the reigning Champion found his rhythm to retake second at the flag after dropping to fourth when his Kawasaki teammate Leon Haslam joined the party.

Davies did enough to ensure he was on the podium for the second full-distance race of the weekend, pipping Haslam to third after some serious pressure was applied by the former WorldSBK runner-up. Alex Lowes rounded out a strong Spanish weekend in fifth, having held a podium place from Laps 5 to 9.

Eugene Laverty claimed top Independent honours, giving his Goeleven Ducati squad their best ever World Superbike race finish in the process with sixth. Jordi Torres put in another impressive race to take seventh after deposing of Michael van der Mark with some super precise moves in the last two laps. Michael Ruben Rinaldi and Sandro Cortese completed the top ten.

Marco Melandri had another lacklustre race, finishing eleventh ahead of Tom Sykes who was still struggling with a lack of horsepower on the all-new BMW S 1000 RR. Leon Camier, Ryuichi Kiyonari and Markus Reiterberger completed the point-scorers, the German taking the final World Championship point despite two off-track excursions.

WorldSSP

Randy Krummenacher took a fourteen-point lead in the FIM Supersport World Championship, overcoming an on-track deficit of over two seconds after a poor start to secure his second race victory of the season, thanks to an exceptional late-braking move at the final corner of the last lap.

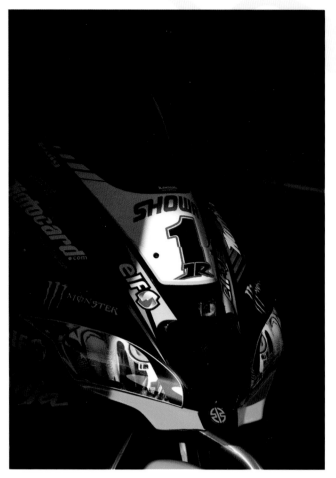

Once again at the sharp end from the very first Free Practice session of the weekend, Krummenacher continued to be the man to beat as WorldSSP arrived in Europe. Seemingly content to follow the pack after he dropped to fourth at the start, Krummenacher was only classified as the leader across the line once… when it mattered on the final lap. The early race pace was dictated by Federico Caricasulo who rode a mature race out front. Thomas Gradinger took the lead of a World Supersport race for the first time in his career on Lap 10 before being overtaken by the #64 and the #3 of Raffaele De Rosa two laps later.

With a lap to go, Krummenacher waited until the final corner before he made his race-winning move, a superbly executed out-breaking manoeuvre at the end of the ultra-fast back straight. Crossing the line 0.094s ahead, the Swiss rider took his second race win of the year from De Rosa, with Caricasulo completing the podium, a further 0.064s a drift.

Thomas Gradinger, who finished the last three races of 2018 in fourth position, was just edged off the podium again after starting from pole position following a stunning lap in Tissot Superpole. Jules Cluzel lost touch with his rivals in the overall Championship standings after finishing fifth, unable to repeat his race performances from the first two flyaway rounds.

Cluzel's Yamaha teammate Corentin Perolari fought hard to beat Kawasaki pairing Lucas Mahias and Hikari Okubo, the three riders locked together from lights out to the flag. Kyle Smith made his first appearance of the year, racing to an encouraging ninth, the Spanish-based Brit finishing ahead of Isaac Viñales and 1.5s behind the battle for sixth. Federico Fuligni achieved a maiden WorldSSP points finish in thirteenth, ensuring a double-points finish for the first time in 2019 for the MV Agusta Reparto Corse squad.

WorldSSP300

With 51 permanent riders signed up for the third season of the FIM Supersport 300 World Championship action, it was necessary to introduce a new format for each weekend. After Free Practice, the two groups of riders, A and B, would compete in two separate Superpole sessions with the thirty fastest times determining the grid on a combined basis. For those outside the top thirty, the Last Chance Race would give the first six over the line the chance to race in the main Sunday encounter.

Manuel González converted his maiden WorldSSP300 pole position to a career-first World Championship win in front of his home fans after an exhilarating eleven-lap season opener at MotorLand Aragón.

Hitting the front early on, González rode the race of his life, taking the twenty-five points after withstanding race-long attacks from within the leading group of eight.
A perfectly timed move on the final lap saw him ease his way to the front where he was able to edge out Hugo de Cancellis - a first-time podium finisher - for second. Scott Deroue completed the podium after muscling his way to the front from fourteenth on the grid, the Dutchman maintaining his podium run at the Spanish venue (winner in 2017, second in 2018).

Jan-Ole Jähnig took fourth, a mere half-second from the win. He finished a fraction ahead of Andy Verdoïa, Victor Steeman and Omar Bonoli; the top seven covered by 0.891s after eleven frantic laps of racing.

Bruno Ieraci was forced to start from the back of the grid after qualifying a strong tenth on his debut. The Italian passed sixteen competitors on the opening lap before continuing to push forward, eventually finishing an impressive eighth. 2018 winner Koen Meuffels and Max Kappler completed the top ten.

Reigning WorldSSP300 Champion Ana Carrasco crashed out of the front-running group as a result of a nudge from Nick Kalinin, after slowing to avoid an incident ahead; she was unhurt. Marc García, the first ever FIM Supersport 300 World Champion, returned to the grid in 2019 after a season out and lowly twenty-fifth at the flag.

There was heartbreak for front row qualifier Galang Hendra Pratama, who crashed out early on after making contact with another rider.

 **TT Circuit Assen**
12 - 14 April

Snow joke –
Álvaro aces Assen

After the postponement of the opening Dutch race because of snow it was a case of back to the future for WorldSBK in Assen, with two feature length races on a Sunday and the cancellation of the Tissot Superpole Race. A reduction to the upper rev limit of the Ducati Panigale V4 R provided what was intended, closer racing and thrilling action. Despite this, Álvaro Bautista equalled the record for consecutive WorldSBK race wins (eleven), thanks to another double victory at the Cathedral of Speed.

WorldSBK Race 1
After taking his third pole position of the year, albeit in a shortened Tissot Superpole qualifying session, Álvaro Bautista took win number ten by three seconds. Controlling things at the front after taking the lead from the start, Bautista was once again in a class of his own despite an inspired challenge in the opening seven laps from BMW-mounted Markus Reiterberger, who had qualified on the front row. Eventual second place man Jonathan Rea took eight laps to muscle his way past 'Reiti' but even he was unable to mount a serious challenge on the #19 who was victorious once again.

Rea clung on to his tenth second-place finish of the season from local hero Michael van der Mark, who delighted the home fans by also making it past the #28 on Lap 10, going on to secure his first podium of 2019.

Behind the runaway top three, Alex Lowes held off a late challenge from Leon Haslam for fourth, the pair overhauling Reiterberger with several laps remaining. Chaz Davies had a lonely race in seventh, the Aragón double podium finisher coming home three seconds ahead of Jordi Torres who took top Independent honours, Toprak Razgatlioglu and Tom Sykes, who was unable to replicate the pace he had during Superpole.

After fighting for the podium in Spain, Eugene Laverty seemed to struggle all weekend in The Netherlands, taking fourteenth at the flag after fending off the attentions of Ryuichi Kiyonari who took the final World Championship point.

Tissot Superpole Race
Race cancelled.

MOTUL DUTCH ROUND

CIRCUIT ASSEN

SBK MOTUL
FIM SUPERBIKE WORLD CHAMPIONSHIP

Race 1

1. **Álvaro Bautista** — 21 laps
2. **Jonathan Rea** — +3.130s
3. **Chaz Davies** — +4.934s

Tissot Superpole Race

- **Race cancelled**

Race 2

1. **Álvaro Bautista** — 21 laps
2. **Michael van der Mark** — +4.688s
3. **Jonathan Rea** — +4.706s

SUPERSPORT
FIM WORLD CHAMPIONSHIP

Race

1. **Federico Caricasulo** — 18 laps
2. **Randy Krummenacher** — +0.032s
3. **Thomas Gradinger** — +0.223s

SUPERSPORT300
FIM WORLD CHAMPIONSHIP

1. **Manuel González** — 12 laps
2. **Scott Deroue** — +0.143s
3. **Jan-Ohle Jähnig** — +.0320s

WorldSBK Race 2

For the first time this year, for five laps at least, Jonathan Rea reminded us why he is a four-time Superbike World Champion. The #1 hit the front from the off thanks to one of the best race starts in the Championship's history, responding to any challenge that came as the leading group of six stayed locked together for the opening half dozen laps.

Rea did all he could but the race-winning move from his arch rival for the 2019 crown, Álvaro Bautista, was inevitable, and on Lap 6 the Spanish rider made his move. Opening up an immediate half second lead over Rea, Álvaro was never headed, romping to his record-equalling eleventh consecutive race win by almost five seconds.

As in Race 1, the battle for the final two places on the podium went down to the wire. Michael van der Mark was in no mood to finish third, the Yamaha rider making some audacious moves which were immediately countered by the #1. With the Dutch crowd on their feet and the fans watching the action at the Paddock Show screaming, 'Magic Michael' pulled off the move of the season to date. Colliding with Rea, the pair were lucky to stay aboard, as van der Mark took the twenty points by 0.018s after another classic Assen photo finish.

Lowes continued his consistent start to the season in fourth, finishing comfortably ahead of Chaz Davies and Markus Reiterberger who secured another top six finish, his best weekend since returning to WorldSBK. Tom Sykes was classified seventh after crossing the line side-by-side with his BMW teammate.

Leon Haslam was disappointed to finish eighth whilst Toprak Razgatlioglu took the best Independent prize after another race-long duel with Jordi Torres. Sandro Cortese's debut season in World Superbike continued with yet more points in eleventh, with Leon Camier coming out on top in a four-way fight for twelfth. Eugene Laverty, Marco Melandri and Michael Ruben Rinaldi completed the point-scorers.

WorldSSP

After starting from pole, Randy Krummenacher lost out on the win in Assen by 0.032s after an explosive final lap saw him outfoxed by his teammate Federico Caricasulo.

With never more than 0.5s between the pair throughout the eighteen-lap encounter, it was a game of chess on two wheels, as the two title contenders were joined at the front by early leader Jules Cluzel. Raffaele De Rosa, Thomas Gradinger and Lucas Mahias were also right in the mix during the opening laps.

A fast-starting Hannes Soomer was up to fourth at the end of Lap 1, the Baltic Bullet gradually fading before crashing on Lap 13. No strong result at Assen for the Estonian this time around.

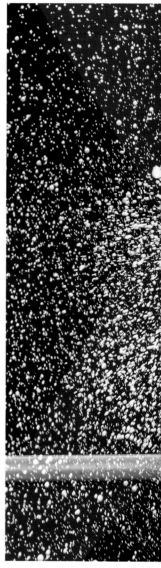

De Rosa also slid out of contention on Lap 12 which slightly split the group, Krummenacher still marginally ahead with only a few laps to go.

A perfectly timed move by Caricasulo gave long-time leader Krummenacher no chance to respond, the Swiss rider having to settle for second at the flag. Thomas Gradinger's threat of a podium had been coming since the last quarter of 2018, and after twenty-nine minutes and forty-eight seconds of intense racing the threat became a reality.
His podium was also the first WorldSSP podium for an Austrian rider in the 21-year history of the series.

Jules Cluzel recovered after losing pace in the middle of the race to finish fourth ahead of compatriot Lucas Mahias, who set the fastest lap of the race on Lap 10, just over half-a-second from his maiden Kawasaki podium. Corentin Perolari took an encouraging top six finish ahead of Hikari Okubo and Isaac Viñales, the trio covered by two tenths of a second as they crossed the line.

Teenager Glenn van Straalen finished a brilliant ninth in only his sixth WorldSSP appearance, whilst Jules Danilo was the top Honda finisher in tenth. Loris Cresson picked up yet more points in thirteenth, the Belgian rider classing the Dutch event as his home race. Rob Hartog finished fourteenth to add two points to his season's tally.

WorldSSP300
Two seconds covered the top seventeen finishers in one of the closest and craziest WorldSSP300 races of all-time.

With positions changing several times a corner, the on-track action was fast and furious, with nine riders holding potential podium places on the official end of lap analysis provided at the end of the race.

Bruno Ieraci overhauled early leaders Jan-Ole Jähnig and Hugo de Cancellis on Lap 4 whilst local rider Scott Deroue made hard work of it, completing the opening lap in ninth before dropping to tenth on Lap 3.

As the field entered the final lap, Ana Carrasco made a bid for glory, the reigning World Champion keen to make up for her first-round exit. With the leading group fanning out through the fast sweeping final sector, a number of riders made contact which resulted in Carrasco and the impressive Ieraci dropping down the order.

It was no holds barred into the final chicane, the scene of many a race-winning and race-ending moves, and with three of the leading four riders either off the track or cutting the chicane completely, there was a lengthy wait until the result was confirmed. González was given the nod ahead of Scott Deroue, after a stunning final lap, and Jähnig climbed onto the podium for the first time in his short World Championship career. Nick Kalinin, De Cancellis, Omar Bonoli, Ieraci, Carrasco, Andy Verdoïa and Victor Steeman completed a top ten that was split by only a second.

2017 World Champion Marc García picked up his first points since returning to the series, in eleventh.

Resurgent Rea doubles up in Imola

Jonathan Rea responded to Álvaro Bautista's dominance by romping to a convincing double win. After eleven consecutive victories, Bautista was finally beaten in Ducati's back yard. Chaz Davies reminded us all that he is one of the fastest Superbike riders on the planet and BMW Motorrad sent out a warning that it's only a matter of time before they are back on the World Superbike podium.

WorldSBK Race 1

Jonathan Rea stormed to his first win of 2019 in a lights-to-flag race that saw him beat Championship leader Álvaro Bautista by 7.8s. The four-time Champion rode the perfect race, easing away at the front to re-ignite his quest for a fifth WorldSBK crown.

Bautista, making his race debut at Imola, used his head to take twenty valuable points for second. The Spanish rider was kept honest for the first half of the race by BMW-mounted Tom Sykes, who following Chaz Davies' opening lap exit, looked comfortable in third. Gapping the pack behind, Sykes suffered a technical problem as the race hit the halfway mark, robbing the German manufacturer of what would have been their first podium since Jerez in 2013.

With Sykes sidelined, the battle for the final podium place was intense. Toprak Razgatlioglu, Michael van der Mark and Leon Haslam were locked together and with all three desperate to come out on top, the fans were treated to some incredible overtakes and some heart-stopping on-track moments. Haslam looked the faster of the trio but ran off-track several times, the reigning BSB Champion eventually finishing fifth. At the flag and after a bit of elbow rubbing, third went to Toprak, the protégé of five-time Supersport World Champion Kenan Sofuoglu taking top Independent honours as well as his third career WorldSBK podium.

Marco Melandri once again showed a consistent race pace, especially in the closing stages, to finish sixth ahead of Alex Lowes who overcame a virus to salvage seventh. Michael Ruben Rinaldi, who suffered a monster crash in Tissot Superpole, took a credible eighth ahead of wildcard and WorldSBK returnee,

PIRELLI ITALIAN ROUND

IMOLA
AUTODROMO INTERNAZIONALE ENZO E DINO FERRARI

FIM SUPERBIKE WORLD CHAMPIONSHIP

Race 1

1 Jonathan Rea — 19 laps
2 Álvaro Bautista — +7.832ss
3 Toprak Razgatlioglu — +19.291s

Tissot Superpole Race

1 Jonathan Rea — 10 laps
2 Chaz Davies — +2.141s
3 Álvaro Bautista — +6.864s

Race 2

- Race cancelled

SUPERSPORT
FIM WORLD CHAMPIONSHIP

Race

1 Randy Krummenacher — 17 laps
2 Federico Caricasulo — +0.234s
3 Raffaele De Rosa — +13.412s

SUPERSPORT300
FIM WORLD CHAMPIONSHIP

- Race cancelled

Lorenzo Zanetti. The sole remaining BMW of Markus Reiterberger finished tenth.

Eugene Laverty's weekend was over before it began, the #50 suffering two broken wrists in an FP1 crash. Successfully operated on, his Goeleven Ducati squad drafted in Tommy Bridewell, the front-running BSB rider who after only a handful of laps in Tissot Superpole took an impressive twelfth position.

Tissot Superpole Race
Intent on making up for the disappointment of Saturday's opening race, Chaz Davies made the best of starts to lead the field from the off. A mistake on the brakes at the end of the opening lap allowed Jonathan Rea and Ducati teammate Álvaro Bautista through, the three riders immediately stretching a gap at the front.

Rea did what he does best by controlling things from the front, and after a handful of laps he had a more than comfortable gap out front. Davies, now understanding how his half wet / half dry set up was working, pulled the pin. He first eased past Bautista and the #7 obliterated the lap record to close to within striking distance of Rea and set up a potential Imola classic. Sadly, the Tissot Superpole Race is only ten laps long and Davies simply ran out of time.

Rea took his seventy-third career win to further underline his name as the most successful WorldSBK rider of all-time. Davies was delighted with his return to front-running pace and the fact he had beaten runaway Championship leader and teammate Bautista for the first time this season. Another podium for Bautista ensured he remained atop the overall standings, albeit with a slightly reduced points advantage of 43. Michael van der Mark, Alex Lowes and Leon Haslam completed the top six.

Toprak Razgatlioglu was top Independent rider for the second time in two races; he finished seventh ahead of Tom Sykes, who had to start from the pit lane following a tyre pressure issue on the grid. The final point went to Jordi Torres.

WorldSBK Race 2
Race Cancelled

WorldSSP
The first visit to Italy this year for the WorldSSP competitors turned into a game of cat and mouse for BARDAHL Evan Bros. Teammates Randy Krummenacher and Federico Caricasulo played mind games with each other throughout the seventeen-lap race. The early threat from Jules Cluzel faded away thanks to a Lap 11 incident that saw his GMT94 Yamaha appear to slow out of the final chicane, it later being revealed that the Frenchman's

foot unintentionally clipped his gear-changer which this season was on the right side of the bike due to the left ankle injury he sustained in Qatar last year. The sudden lack of acceleration from the #16 took out 2017 World Champion Lucas Mahias, who was having another strong race for Kawasaki Puccetti Racing, and Thomas Gradinger who was proving that his maiden WorldSSP podium at Assen last time out was no fluke.

The incident set free Krummenacher and Caricasulo, the pair pushing each other to the limit. A new race strategy after the last round in The Netherlands saw Krummenacher move aside to give his young teammate the chance to lead the race, Randy content to follow in his wheel tracks. The fastest lap of the race for Championship leader Krummenacher on the penultimate lap set up a thrilling finale. With each rider clearly stronger at different parts of the circuit, it was a one-lap shootout for glory.

Caricasulo went deep on the brakes into Tosa but still the #21 sat behind, waiting for his moment which came a handful

of corners later on the exit of the Variante Alta. Still not home and dry, Krummenacher braked later than normal into the final chicane which compromised his exit giving a last glimmer of hope to home hero Caricasulo, but it was too little, too late. Krummenacher crossed the line to win his third race of the season and in doing so, extended his lead in the overall standings to twenty-two points. Caricasulo took second after being affected by a technical problem on the final lap, thirteen seconds ahead of compatriot Raffaele De Rosa, who put his MV Agusta Reparto Corse machine on the podium for the second time this season.

A last lap highside for multiple CIV Supersport Champion Massimo Roccoli, who was fighting for fourth, brought out the red flag meaning only the top five actually completed the full race distance.

Hikari Okubo, the surprise of the season for many, finished fourth (his best ever result in World Championship racing) from former WorldSSP race winner Ayrton Badovini who took his best result of the year to date. Isaac Viñales returned to the top six.

Cluzel, who had managed to stay aboard in the earlier melee, salvaged nine points for seventh at the flag, ahead of the recovering Lucas Mahias' Kawasaki and the Hondas of Hannes Soomer and Peter Sebestyen which completed the top ten.

WorldSSP300
Race Cancelled

CIRCUITO DE JEREZ

‹‹‹ *Circuito de Jerez - Ángel Nieto 7 - 9 June*

Michael works his magic as Álvaro takes a tumble

A lap record-breaking, incident-packed weekend in sunny Spain ultimately resulted in more success for Álvaro Bautista. World Champion Jonathan Rea started from the back of the grid in the Tissot Superpole Race and Michael van der Mark gave Yamaha their first win of 2019. It ended with a war of words and a grid penalty for Marco Melandri that he would have to serve at the next round in Misano.

WorldSBK Race 1

After dispensing with the threat from Jonathan Rea at Turn 5 on the opening lap, Álvaro Bautista romped home to secure his twelfth win from fourteen starts by seven seconds at the flag. Predictably, this sent the thousands of fans in the Fan Zone at Jerez into a frenzy as he showered them during the podium ceremony. An emotional Bautista dedicated the victory to his grandfather who had recently passed away.

Behind the runaway #19 Ducati, Michael van der Mark showed his early weekend pace was no fluke as he too overhauled Rea, making the decisive move for second on Lap 9 before opening up a comfortable margin of almost four seconds over his pursuers by Lap 15.

With one lap to go all eyes were on the intense battle that had raged throughout between the clearly struggling #1 of Jonathan Rea and #22 of Alex Lowes, who looked certain to give Yamaha their first double podium of the year. However, another Turn 13 incident would get the whole paddock talking. Rea wanted the final podium spot and after breaking later than usual he dived to the inside, only to collide with the unsuspecting #22, who was sent tumbling into the gravel. Rea crossed the line third only to be given a post-race penalty which dropped him to fourth, elevating top Independent rider Marco Melandri into the sixteen-point position. Not only this, but a second penalty for Rea saw him demoted to the back of the grid for Sunday's Tissot Superpole Race. Toprak Razgatlioglu and Tom Sykes completed the top six whilst the top ten was rounded out by Chaz Davies, Sandro Cortese (who overcame a poor start to finish eighth), Leon Haslam and Michael Ruben Rinaldi. Loris Baz picked up four

SBK MOTUL
FIM SUPERBIKE WORLD CHAMPIONSHIP

Race 1

1	Álvaro Bautista	20 laps
2	Michael van der Mark	+7.119s
3	Marco Melandri	+19.951s

Tissot Superpole Race

1	Álvaro Bautista	10 laps
2	Michael van der Mark	+2.743s
3	Marco Melandri	+2.954s

Race 2

1	Michael van der Mark	18 laps (red flag)
2	Jonathan Rea	+3.548s
3	Toprak Razgatlioglu	minus one sector

SUPERSPORT
FIM WORLD CHAMPIONSHIP

Race

1	Federico Caricasulo	19 laps
2	Randy Krummenacher	+0.968s
3	Jules Cluzel	+1.346s

SUPERSPORT300
FIM WORLD CHAMPIONSHIP

1	Marc García	11 laps
2	Scott Deroue	+0.054s
3	Ana Carrasco	+0.167s

points on his return to racing, the Frenchman finishing twelfth. Tommy Bridewell, again deputising for the still injured Eugene Laverty took fourteenth, several seconds ahead of Alessandro Delbianco who scored points for the third time in his WorldSBK career.

Tissot Superpole Race

It was anything but an unlucky thirteenth race win for Álvaro Bautista, who doubled-up on home soil to give him 12+1 victories at the circuit now appropiately named after thirteen-time World Champion Ángel Nieto.

Following a recent test at Misano and buoyed by his first race podium, albeit thanks to Rea's penalty, Marco Melandri reminded everyone that he should not be overlooked as he continued his adaption to his four-cylinder Yamaha. The #33 ran a strong second, matching Bautista's pace in the early stages before being passed by Michael van der Mark on Lap 8. The Dutchman and the Italian ensured that there were two blue machines in Parc Ferme, crossing line just 0.2s apart.

Insult was added to injury for Rea who was sent to the back of the grid for Sunday's Tissot Superpole Race as part of his Race 1 penalty. A cautious start saw him move gradually forward as the race progressed. He eventually finished fourth, a mere 1.7s from the podium after a couple of late race passes on former teammate and 2013 World Champion Tom Sykes, who had been fighting for a potential podium place in the early laps, and current KRT teammate Leon Haslam who ran third on track until Lap 4.

Toprak Razgatlioglu finished seventh after a pretty lonely race. The final two points-scoring positions were taken by Jordi Torres, who made up for his Race 1 retirement by finishing eighth, and Sandro Cortese, who battled with the Spanish rider throughout but was unable to make a pass. There was further heartbreak for Alex Lowes who crashed out on Lap 4 whilst fighting inside the top six.

WorldSBK Race 2

Michael van der Mark became the third race winner of the season after getting the better of Jonathan Rea on Lap 7, after an early exit from runaway Championship leader Álvaro Bautista, who crashed at Turn 1 on Lap 2. The tense race-long duel also involved Toprak Razgatlioglu in the opening few laps before the talented Turkish rider lost touch with the leading pair. He settled for third after his nearest rivals Chaz Davies and Marco Melandri collided and crashed at speed at Turn 5 onto the back straight on Lap 6. Each blaming the other for their trip into the gravel, it was Melandri who was deemed to be at fault by the stewards, as they imposed a six-place grid penalty on the Italian for the Tissot Superpole Race in Misano. Rea and van der Mark swapped positions repeatedly before the Yamaha-mounted Dutchman eased away to win by 2.7s after a red flag with only a couple of laps to go (due to gravel on the circuit following a crash for Ryuichi Kiyonari). The Championship took a new twist, with now arguably only three riders in contention as the season headed towards the halfway point.

Rea admitted in Parc Ferme that he had 'given up' fighting for the win after several slides and near crashes, opting to bank the twenty points for second, knowing all too well that with Bautista scoring zero it could make the difference at the end of the season.

ACERBIS SPANISH ROUND

Circuito de Jerez - Ángel Nieto 2019

Toprak Razgatlioglu once again showed why many teams have the talented Turkish rider on their radar, the 22-year-old taking a convincing second podium in as many events, finishing more than five seconds ahead of Michael Ruben Rinaldi who rode the race of his young WorldSBK career to finish fourth: a great birthday present for Marco 'Barni' Barnabo, his team manager.

Leon Haslam finished fifth after responding to the constant on-track attacks from Sandro Cortese, Jordi Torres and Tom Sykes. The quintet was separated by only 2.6s after twenty hard-fought laps – a glimpse of what the remaining races could have in store, perhaps?

Loris Baz delighted Ten Kate Racing with a top ten finish in only their third race with Yamaha, the Frenchman finished several seconds ahead of Tommy Bridewell who put in another impressive performance to finish tenth.
In a race of attrition, Leandro Mercado, Markus Reiterberger and Yuki Takahashi were the final point-scorers in eleventh to thirteenth, respectively. Bautista rejoined from the pits on a repaired Ducati, but was not classified as he failed to complete two-thirds of the scheduled laps.

WorldSSP
The BARDAHL Evan Bros Yamaha duo of Federico Caricasulo and Randy Krummenacher took their third one-two finish of the year and in succession. The Italian got the better of his Swiss rival to reduce the points gap in the overall standings to seventeen points after another nail-biting nineteen-lap WorldSSP encounter.

Despite breaking the outright lap record in Tissot Superpole, Caricasulo was stripped of pole position after completing the lap whilst multiple yellow flags were shown. That gave the upper hand to Krummenacher, who had also set a lap record worthy time to initially take P1 on the grid.

As the lights went out, we saw the welcome return of 2017 World Champion Lucas Mahias, who converted his front row start to the race lead, a position he held until Lap 3 when the Yamaha assault began.

#21 from #64 seemed to be the way it would go until Caricasulo showed his hand on Lap 12, but Krummenacher had other ideas and immediately responded. The pair were taken slightly by surprise on Lap 16 by a charging Jules Cluzel who, after crashing at high speed on Saturday, was working his way towards the front. A mid-race fight with Mahias only momentarily halted his ascent, the dicing French duo opting to work together to close down the leaders. The strategy worked and when Cluzel took the lead it was like throwing a red rag to a bull. Despite this consecutive lap records on the penultimate and the last lap gave Caricasulo the win by less than a second, Krummenacher was also under the lap record and despite also getting the better of Cluzel, he was left with just too much to do.

platform to remind everyone he had lost none of his speed. The 19-year-old Spaniard qualified second before showing that using your head and being in the right place at the right time is how you win in WorldSSP300.

Ensuring he was in the leading group, García led at the end of Lap 4 before being pushed back to sixth at the end of Lap 9. With Ana Carrasco heading the pack into the final corner, García - who had impressively worked his way back into contention - made his move. Edging last year's Champion out of the way, the #42 took his first win of the season by 0.054s. García's move on Carrasco gave just enough room for Scott Deroue to sneak through into second position, ahead of the #1 Kawasaki rider, who took her first podium of the season. Championship leader Manuel González finished fourth ahead of Andy Verdoïa and Galang Hendra Pratama; pole-sitter Victor Steeman could only manage twelfth. He crossed the line 1.8s from the win in what was another stunning race that saw all of the point scorers split by 2.5s at the flag.

With Saturday's nail-biting lights-to-flag on-track action still on everyone's mind, Sunday's race delivered even more with the top four riders crossing the line in a reduced seven-lap thriller by a quarter of a second, the closest podium in WorldSSP300 history.

Sunday's race was shortened to seven laps after an initial opening lap crash that claimed five riders including Championship contender Scott Deroue, who was unable to avoid the fallen bike at Turn 2. He made the restart but could only finish twenty-third after having to start from the back of the grid for the restart.

Manuel González had clearly learned from the events of 24 hours earlier, positioning himself perfectly for the final sprint to the line. After more than twenty lead changes, González claimed his third race win of the year from García, who jumped up to third overall in the standings thanks to his front-running rides. Carrasco again finished third whilst Victor Steeman, buoyed by his first ever World Championship pole position on Saturday, narrowly missed his first ever podium finish. He finished fifth, just ahead of KTM teammate Jan-Ole Jähnig and just behind Galang Hendra Pratama, who celebrated a few metres too early before immediately getting back behind the bubble once he had realised his mistake.

Bruno Ieraci put in another stunning performance in the opening encounter, charging from 31st on the grid to sixth on Lap 11. He sadly slid out of contention a corner from home. In the shortened seven-lap race on Sunday, he was once again able to scythe through the pack, taking twelfth in a photo finish.

Twentieth at the end of the opening lap, Beatriz Neila was ecstatic and rightly as she clinched her first ever World Championship points with thirteenth-place finish.

Cluzel clung on to third, his first podium finish since his win in Thailand. He claimed after the race that he needs to find something - and fast - if he is to remain a contender for the title.

Thomas Gradinger put in another front-running performance to claim fourth, a couple of bike lengths ahead of Raffaele De Rosa who had been running third until Lap 12 when he was unable to increase his pace.

Mahias took sixth, more than twelve seconds ahead of teammate Hikari Okubo who kept out of trouble to beat Isaac Viñales, Corentin Perolari and Peter Sebestyen, who were eighth to tenth respectively.

Maria Herrera took more points in fourteenth whilst, on the final lap, Rob Hartog stole what would have been a first World Championship point this season for German rider Christian Stange.

WorldSSP300
Following the race cancellation in Imola the WorldSSP300 contenders had two races in Jerez. 2017 Supersport 300 World Champion Marc García used the Jerez double-header as a

Rea rains supreme after Bautista's Misano mistake

A second Race 2 mistake from Álvaro Bautista in as many events saw Jonathan Rea slash the points deficit to his Spanish rival to sixteen points as the first half of the season concluded at Misano. After triumphing in the first wet race of the year on Saturday, the five-time Champion elect recovered from a rare mistake of his own on Sunday morning that allowed the pendulum to swing from green to red once again, before ensuring his title challenge was well and truly back on track by the time the final Superbike chequered flag of the weekend was waved.

WorldSBK Race 1

After a sweltering opening day of on-track action that saw Michael van der Mark atop the overall combined classification, conditions couldn't have been more different when the lights went out for Race 1. Overnight rain and a torrential downpour saw many of the leading riders - including Championship leader Álvaro Bautista - signal that conditions were not good for racing, which resulted in a short delay before the opening encounter began. With only a couple of laps completed, the heavens opened once again, bringing out the red flags and a reduced re-run of 18 laps. It was a case of third time not so lucky for Alex Lowes, who after overhauling early leader Jonathan Rea and building a comfortable lead of over two seconds, crashed out at speed but was thankfully unhurt. That left Rea out in front with an impressive margin of over five seconds from Tom Sykes who converted a front row start to give BMW their first WorldSBK front row since Portugal six years ago.

An intermittent electrical problem curtailed any chance that Chaz Davies had of a podium finish. He lost touch with the fight for third, eventually finishing fifth. His teammate Álvaro Bautista secured another podium, albeit helped by Lowes' exit and his own teammate's misfortune. Loris Baz finished fourth in only his third race back in the Championship. The all-new Ten Kate Racing Yamaha partnership picking up top Independent honours too. Chaz Davies and Marco Melandri rounded out the top six with Sandro Cortese, Yuki Takahashi, Lorenzo Zanetti and Leandro Mercado completing the top ten.

PATA RIVIERA DI RIMINI ROUND

Misano
World Circuit
Marco Simoncelli

FIM SUPERBIKE WORLD CHAMPIONSHIP

Race 1

1	Jonathan Rea	18 laps
2	Tom Sykes	+3.692s
3	Álvaro Bautista	+7.756s

Tissot Superpole Race

1	Álvaro Bautista	10 laps
2	Alex Lowes	+7.261s
3	Leon Haslam	+9.154s

Race 2

1	Jonathan Rea	21 laps
2	Toprak Razgatlioglu	+0.381s
3	Leon Haslam	+5.880s

SUPERSPORT
FIM WORLD CHAMPIONSHIP

1	Randy Krummenacher	19 laps
2	Federico Caricasulo	+0.084s
3	Lucas Mahias	+0.161s

SUPERSPORT300
FIM WORLD CHAMPIONSHIP

1	Ana Carrasco	13 laps
2	Manuel González	+0.822s
3	Andy Verdoïa	+0.965s

There were first World Superbike Championship points for Samuele Cavalieri in thirteenth. Michael van der Mark was ruled out of all three races after suffering a horrific highside in the final seconds of Friday's FP2. Diagnosed with a broken wrist and a couple of bruised ribs (initially expected to have been fractured), the Dutchman was likely to miss the UK and US rounds.

Tissot Superpole Race

Álvaro Bautista equalled the record for rookie rider wins in their first season after taking his 14th victory of the year and making things look easy once again on a Sunday morning. Winning by 7.261s from Alex Lowes, who was back on the podium after four races on the floor, and Leon Haslam, who gave Kawasaki their 400th WorldSBK podium after a fine performance in third.

Jonathan Rea crashed on Lap 8, throwing away what was a safe looking podium. Remounting after his spill in which the bike rolled over the top of him, he salvaged fifth behind Toprak Razgatlioglu, who put in another fine performance in fourth, a mere quarter of a second behind Haslam.

Marco Melandri and Michael Ruben Rinaldi had an all Italian duel throughout for sixth, the veteran #33 edging his younger compatriot by half-a-second at the flag. Michele Pirro and Leandro Mercado picked up the final points on offer in eighth and ninth, respectively.

Tom Sykes was robbed of a first back-to-back BMW podium after suffering an engine-related technical problem on the final lap.

WorldSBK Race 2

Toprak Razgatlioglu pushed Jonathan Rea to the limit in arguably the best race of the season thus far, eventually finishing second after an intense race-long duel ended with a frantic final lap battle that saw the four-time Champion come out on top.

When the lights went out Álvaro Bautista hit the front almost immediately, but the Spanish rider's quest for win number fifteen ended as quickly as it had begun as he slid out of contention on Lap 2, just as he had done in Jerez a fortnight earlier. He remounted to finish fourteenth.

With Álvaro on the floor many would have thought it would have been an easy ride for Jonathan Rea, but they were wrong. After podiums in Imola and Jerez, Toprak Razgatlioglu was fast becoming the rider to watch and that was certainly the case in Misano.

Seemingly glued to Rea's rear wheel in the early laps, Toprak made his move, hitting the front on Lap 5 before resisting the threat of retaliation from the #1. Rea eased back into the lead on Lap 18, but the protégé of five-time Supersport

World Champion Kenan Sofuoglu wasn't finished yet, sizing up Rea seemingly at every corner with only a few laps to go.
As the pair started their final 2.6 miles, Razgatlioglu was in no mood for playing second fiddle surprising Rea with an outbraking move at Quercia corner that Rea himself would have been proud of. Rea responded immediately, clinging on after another spirited assault from the #54 which had the crowd on their feet.

Leon Haslam made it an all-green podium after fending off Alex Lowes for third. It was only the second time in World Superbike history that Kawasaki bikes had locked-out the podium.

Michael Ruben Rinaldi picked up his second best result of the season in fifth after overhauling Tom Sykes, who had to resort an older spec BMW engine after his earlier Tissot Superpole Race misfortune.

The rest of the top ten finishers had relatively lonely races with Chaz Davies coming home seventh, three seconds ahead of Michele Pirro, who in turn was five seconds ahead of Lorenzo Zanetti, with Jordi Torres a couple of seconds further back.

WorldSSP
Misano served up the most intense on-track duel of the season as Randy Krummenacher and Federico Caricasulo showed once again that there are no team orders in their squad.

As the lights went out, it was former World Champion Lucas Mahias who hit the front, where he would stay until Lap 3 when Krummenacher made his move. The #21 rider was immediately followed by his teammate Caricasulo who knew the biggest threat would come from his Swiss rival. The remaining laps were like watching a pan of water being brought to the boil: you know it's going to happen, but the question is when. The answer came as the leading trio, still separated by the proverbial cigarette paper, began the last lap. A brilliant late braking manoeuvre from Caricasulo took Krummenacher by surprise to give the Italian the advantage, but the Championship leader was far from done and responded with an aggressive retaking of the lead a handful of corners from home. Side-by-side through the

penultimate corner, the pair touched as Caricasulo made one final bid for glory, only to be denied by the determined Krummenacher, who slammed the door firmly in his face to take his fourth win of the season.

Lucas Mahias had a grandstand seat of the action in front of him and almost capitalised, missing the win by only 0.061s at the line.

Jules Cluzel ended Lap 1 fourth and stayed there, the Frenchman unable to move into podium contention despite latching onto the group in the early stages. Hikari Okubo rode to fifth ahead of Lorenzo Gabellini who took a very impressive sixth. Hannes Soomer was once again the top Honda in seventh ahead of Kevin Manfredi, Thomas Gradinger and multiple Italian Supersport Champion Massimo Roccoli, making it three wildcard riders inside the top ten.

Federico Fuligni picked up points on his MV Agusta in eleventh as did Mattia Casadei, with the young Italian taking the single point on offer for fifteenth on his first ride in the series.

WorldSSP300

Ana Carrasco won her first race of the season to move into second position in the overall standings after a perfectly judged move with a little over a lap giving her the edge over the Championship leader Manuel González. Behind the two Spanish riders, there was a first WorldSSP300 podium for France's Andy Verdoïa, who remained part of the leading group throughout. Verdoïa pipped Galang Hendra Pratama for the final spot on the podium in a last lap drag race out of the final corner. The gap between the pair was 0.097s, with Victor Steeman only half a second behind in fifth and wildcard rider Emanuele Vocino finishing in a very credible sixth.

At the front, the race itself was typical WorldSSP300, although the top six were able to break clear of a lonely Scott Deroue who kept his head down to finish seventh after a poor qualifying.

PROSECCO DOC UK ROUND

◀◀◀ Donington Park
5 - 7 July

All change at the top after Rea's Donington triple

'**C**onsistency is key' is a phrase that has often been overused in motorsport circles but, as the WorldSBK paddock neared the summer break, it was one that had never been truer. A first triple win of the season for Jonathan Rea, coupled with his early season consistency had swung the pendulum from red to green. With Álvaro Bautista suffering another early race crash, the title race was blown wide open.

WorldSBK Race 1

With rain falling, the opening race of the weekend got underway with Jonathan Rea taking the early lead. Never headed throughout the 23-lap race, Rea took the win from Tom Sykes, who was also never headed, the former World Champion holding second from start to finish.

Leon Haslam took the final podium place in third after getting the better of wet weather specialist Loris Baz who had been running inside the top three until Lap 6.

In what was a very spread out race, Alex Lowes took fifth from Leandro Mercado, who equalled his best ever WorldSBK result in sixth. Peter Hickman, deputising for Markus Reiterberger (who was suffering from a virus), rode a smart race to seventh ahead of Michael van der Mark.

Alessandro Delbianco had shown in earlier rounds just how fast he was in damp conditions and he got to show us once again at Donington Park. The Italian youngster is relishing the opportunity to learn from the World's best but after Race 1 in the UK there are many that could learn from him. A high-speed, Randy Mamola-esque side-saddle recovery not once but twice at the infamous Craner Curves. Staying aboard his Honda on both occasions, Delbianco finished ninth ahead of Chaz Davies to record his best ever WorldSBK finish.

Ryuichi Kiyonari finished eleventh, ahead of Michael Ruben Rinaldi and Toprak Razgatlioglu, who aren't fans of wet conditions. Marco Melandri was the last classified rider in fourteenth, the Italian lapped by the flying Rea.

DoningtonPark

SBK MOTUL
FIM SUPERBIKE WORLD CHAMPIONSHIP

Race 1

1	**Jonathan Rea**	23 laps
2	**Tom Sykes**	+11.348s
3	**Leon Haslam**	+23.071s

Tissot Superpole Race

1	**Jonathan Rea**	7 laps (Red Flag)
2	**Toprak Razgatlioglu**	+1.174s
3	**Leon Haslam**	+1.666s

Race 2

1	**Jonathan Rea**	23 laps
2	**Toprak Razgatlioglu**	+0.365s
3	**Álvaro Bautista**	+5.930s

SUPERSPORT
FIM WORLD CHAMPIONSHIP

1	**Jules Cluzel**	20 laps
2	**Federico Caricasulo**	+0.114s
3	**Lucas Mahias**	+0.436s

SUPERSPORT300
FIM WORLD CHAMPIONSHIP

1	**Kevin Sabatucci**	13 laps
2	**Andy Verdoïa**	+0.239s
3	**Nick Kalinin**	+0.447s

Álvaro Bautista was running fifth when he crashed heavily at Starkey's on Lap 11.

Tissot Superpole Race

A red flag as the leaders started Lap 7 ended what was shaping up to be a thrilling climax between former teammates Jonathan Rea and Tom Sykes, who was pushing hard for his first BMW win. Early leader Sykes looked comfortable on track after surrendering an early race lead to Rea, but any hope of victory was taken away following a multi-rider incident at the Melbourne Hairpin triggered by an engine failure for his stand in teammate Peter Hickman which left the race track coated with oil, with several riders on the floor and a red flag shown. The result was declared, but there was one more dramatic twist awaiting.

Under red flag conditions, the leading riders approached the incident zone. Sykes hit the oil that had been spilt and went down, luckily avoiding the marshals that were busy clearing the debris and thankfully without injury. As Rea, Sykes and Razgatlioglu celebrated in Parc Ferme, Leon Haslam's Kawasaki was wheeled in and Sykes' BMW removed. The reason? Sykes hadn't ridden his bike to the Parc Ferme within five minutes of the race stoppage, as stated in the Sporting Regulations. Rules are rules and Haslam was credited with third behind a promoted Razgatlioglu and winner Rea, and all-Kawasaki podium.

Álvaro Bautista had been on the back of the leading group and was classified fourth ahead of Loris Baz and Alex Lowes. Chaz Davies, Michael van der Mark and Jordi Torres completed the top nine.

WorldSBK Race 2

Twelve months ago, Toprak Razgatlioglu stunned the WorldSBK paddock by beating Jonathan Rea at Donington Park and this time, the fight between the pair wasn't for second place: it was for the win.

Although ultimately it was Rea who took the spoils to claim a first triple win of the season, it was Razgatlioglu who was once again the rider to push the four-time Champion to his limit, Rea's winning margin less than 0.4s at the flag.

Rea vs. Toprak is becoming a regular occurrence in WorldSBK this year and, after the young Turk hit the front on Lap 3, the stage was set for another classic Champion vs. Pretender duel.
The dicing duo's pace pulled them clear of the field, with Rea retaking the lead on Lap 6 only to lose it again two laps later. Four laps of running second

gave Rea enough of an understanding of where he was stronger, the Northern Irishman making the race-winning move on Lap 12.

Álvaro Bautista kept his title hopes alive with another podium finish, although had the race run a lap or two more, it may well have been another story. Alex Lowes showed incredible pace in the final three laps to overhaul Leon Haslam and close the gap to the #19 to 0.404s at the flag.

Haslam took fifth from Loris Baz whose pace in the dry for the new Ten Kate Yamaha squad is increasing all of the time. Tom Sykes was unable to replicate his earlier pace. He finished seventh, comfortably ahead of Michael van der Mark who defied the odds taking eighth, ensuring a triple-points finish despite riding with a broken wrist. Chaz Davies and Marco Melandri had lonely races to complete the top ten.

Peter Hickman finished a credible eleventh whilst Alessandro Delbianco backed up his wet Race 1 top ten with another points finish in the dry; he finished fifteenth.

WorldSSP

It was World Supersport action at its best from lights to flag at Donington Park, the leading group of four eventually crossing the line eight tenths of a second apart after an exhilarating 20-lap race.

Cluzel worked his way to the front having seemingly been content to follow early leader Lucas Mahias for the first thirteen laps. Once out front, though, the #16 looked comfortable until Federico Caricasulo also found a way past Mahias and closed him down. A last lap lunge gave the Italian the lead for a split second, Cluzel immediately cutting back with a perfectly executed retaking of the lead on the exit of the Melbourne Loop.

Jules Cluzel clung on to win for the second time in 2019 (his first victory since Thailand) to re-ignite his Championship fight. The Frenchman headed into the summer break 41 points adrift of Randy Krummenacher, who held a 15-point advantage over teammate Federico Caricasulo. Lucas Mahias took the final podium spot in third for the second time in as many races.

The Championship leader claimed to have shown everyone that he is the fastest rider on the grid this year and is still the one to beat for the title. A storming ride from tenth on the grid to fourth following a mixed up Tissot Superpole session on

Saturday saw most riders complete only two flying laps before the rain came.

Raffaele De Rosa was back in the points in fifth but was lucky to finish there after a last lap attempt to take the eleven points position went wrong for Hannes Soomer. The Estonian rider crashed out of what would have been a career-best result less than twenty seconds from the flag. Thomas Gradinger finished sixth ahead of reigning British Champion and former WorldSSP Podium finisher Jack Kennedy who was wildcarding. Corentin Perolari, Brad Jones (who was also making a wildcard appearance) and former race winner Ayrton Badovini completed the top ten.

Hikari Okubo started strong but slipped to thirteenth behind Rob Hartog, who was back in the points. Fellow Dutchman Jaimie van Sikkelerus was also back in the points in fourteenth ahead of his teammate Soomer, who remounted to take the final World Championship point.

WorldSSP300
The Championship could have been blown wide open at Donington after runaway Championship leader Manuel González suffered a dislocated shoulder during Tissot Superpole which ruled him out of Sunday's race. Luckily for him, his nearest rivals Marc García, Scott Deroue and Ana Carrasco also all left the UK with zero points after suffering a technical problem, a crash in the Last Chance Race and a crash in the Main Race, respectively.

A mixed grid after rain on Saturday paved the way for one of the most unpredictable and incident-packed World Supersport 300 race of all-time, with two of the podium finishers starting lower than thirtieth.

Ton Kawakami secured a first pole position and Andy Verdoïa second but the teammates were demoted to the back of the grid for tyre pressure infringements which left Galang Hendra Pratama alone on row one as the lights went out.

The carnage began almost immediately after Mika Pérez wiped out the luckless

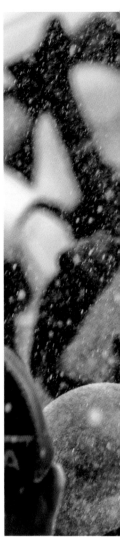

Dorren Lorreiro just metres into the race after veering across the track as the tightly-bunched pack headed towards Redgate Corner. Spaniard Pérez was given a ride through penalty for the incident.

All eyes were on Andy Verdoïa, who passed half the field on the opening lap to amazingly run fourth on the road by Lap 4.

With the top seven well clear of the chasing pack, Kevin Sabatucci took the win from Andy Verdoïa and Nick Kalinin in the most mixed up race result of the season. Two of the podium finishers had started from thirtieth or lower on the grid.

Victor Steeman and Jan-Ole Jähnig finished fourth and fifth respectively with Dion Otten taking sixth, a second from the win on his return to racing action following an early season spill. Oliver Konig delighted team owner and former WorldSBK podium finisher Jakub Smrz with a season's best result of sevent.

Australian Tom Bramich secured his first World Championship points finish in tenth.

75

WeatherTech Raceway Laguna Seca
12 - 14 July

Highs and Laguna
lows for Ducati

What had been a 61-point deficit became an 81-point advantage for Jonathan Rea after the annual visit to WeatherTech Raceway Laguna Seca. His nearest Championship rival Álvaro Bautista suffered a triple zero score, to potentially handing the #1 a fifth WorldSBK crown.

WorldSBK Race 1
Jonathan Rea won the opening US race of 2019 after a lights-to-flag display saw him beat a rejuvenated Chaz Davies by 5.693s. Toprak Razgatlioglu inherited third on Lap 5 after Álvaro Bautista crashed out of the lead battle. Bautista's demise came after setting a new lap record, the Spaniard claiming afterwards that he didn't know why he had crashed.

Tom Sykes finished a well deserved fourth, the 2013 WorldSBK Champion revealing post-race that he had gambled with a rear tyre choice for the opening encounter. Alex Lowes took fifth after a race long duel with Jordi Torres whose mid-season pace reminded the ardent fans that he still possesses the talent to run at the front. Lowes made his move with five laps to go, denying Torres a return to the top five for the first time since Imola 2018.

Loris Baz edged factory Yamaha rider Michael van der Mark, who was still riding with the wrist injury sustained in Misano. Marco Melandri and compatriot Michael Ruben Rinaldi (on his Laguna debut) finished ninth and tenth.

If awards were given for sheer bravery and determination to ride through the pain barrier then, hands down, they would have all gone to Eugene Laverty who put in a heroic performance, racing to eleventh despite suffering much pain with the right wrist he broke at Imola (his left now fully recovered). Leandro Mercado took twelfth ahead of an ecstatic Alessandro Delbianco; the Italian passing reigning Supersport World Champion Sandro Cortese for thirteenth. The returning Markus Reiterberger finished fifteenth after an off-track excursion.

Tissot Superpole Race
The addition of the ten-lap Tissot Superpole Race at each WorldSBK round this year has really changed the dynamic of the series, the short races providing drama and excitement

GEICO U.S. ROUND

WeatherTech® Raceway
LAGUNA SECA

FIM SUPERBIKE WORLD CHAMPIONSHIP

Race 1

1 **Jonathan Rea** — 25 laps
2 **Chaz Davies** — +5.693s
3 **Toprak Razgatlioglu** — +12.721s

Tissot Superpole Race

1 **Jonathan Rea** — 8 laps
2 **Chaz Davies** — +2.533s
3 **Tom Sykes** — +3.641s

Race 2

1 **Chaz Davies** — 25 laps
2 **Jonathan Rea** — +3.333s
3 **Toprak Razgatlioglu** — +11.658s

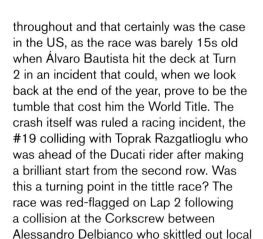

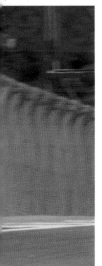

throughout and that certainly was the case in the US, as the race was barely 15s old when Álvaro Bautista hit the deck at Turn 2 in an incident that could, when we look back at the end of the year, prove to be the tumble that cost him the World Title. The crash itself was ruled a racing incident, the #19 colliding with Toprak Razgatlioglu who was ahead of the Ducati rider after making a brilliant start from the second row. Was this a turning point in the tittle race? The race was red-flagged on Lap 2 following a collision at the Corkscrew between Alessandro Delbianco who skittled out local hero and wildcard rider JD Beach.

A shortened race of eight laps began minus the three aforementioned riders, with Jonathan Rea hitting the front from the off. Never being shown a wheel, Rea took the win from a jubilant Chaz Davies whose return to form continued. Tom Sykes took the final podium place after running third throughout.

Toprak Razgatlioglu made an unbelievable pass around the outside of Leon Haslam on the approach to the Corkscrew on Lap 6. He clung on to finish fourth with Haslam fifth, ahead of Alex Lowes who ran sixth throughout.

The final points-scorers were Loris Baz, Jordi Torres and Leandro Mercado.

WorldSBK Race 2

Chaz Davies reminded the WorldSBK paddock that he still knows how to win races after taking a first win of the season and his first on the all-new Panigale V4 R in Race 2. Getting the holeshot, the #7 fought immediately with Jonathan Rea whose late lunge at Turn 5 failed to give him the lead.

With little to separate them, the initial half dozen laps were intriguing, everyone waiting to see when Rea would make his move. The move never came, though, Davies surprising everyone with his consistent race pace to open up a comfortable two-second lead by Lap 13.

Continuing to stretch the gap at the front, the Ducati rider crossed the line to take an emotional 30th career WorldSBK win by 3.333s. Post-race, the Welshman cited important chassis changes made between Friday's first and second practice sessions as the key, and firmly believed the modifications would be transferable for other circuits, also relishing a test at Portimão before the next round of the Championship at the Portuguese circuit.

Rea took another twenty points after another impressive ride to second whilst Toprak Razgatlioglu, who was fast becoming a podium regular, took his ninth career top three finish.

Alex Lowes rode the wheels off his Yamaha to take fourth and, with it, moved into third place overall in the World Championship standings. A fraction of a second behind, Tom Sykes took eleven points for a fifth-place finish into the summer break, the former World Champion showing once again that BMW are back on the World Superbike grid with one clear intention and that was to win.

Leon Haslam took sixth, unable to challenge the top five (riding with a broken thumb following a Corkscrew crash in Race 1) but comfortably ahead of Loris Baz, Jordi Torres, Marco Melandri (on his last ever US appearance since announcing his retirement at the end of 2019) and Michael Ruben Rinaldi.

Leandro Mercado got the better of Eugene Laverty, Markus Reiterberger and Sandro Cortese, whilst Ryuichi Kiyonari denied JD Beach a WorldSBK point after passing the sole American on the grid with four laps to go.

Whilst Ducati were on one hand celebrating, they were despairing on the other after Álvaro Bautista pulled out of the race on Lap 3, the Spaniard in pain after separating the acromioclavicular joint in his left shoulder during the earlier Tissot Superpole Race spill.

《《《 *Autódromo Internacional do Algarve 6 - 8 September*

ACERBIS PORTUGUESE ROUND

All to play for after last lap thrills in Portimão

The summer break was long, but it was worth the wait. Racing resumed in the scorching heat of the Portuguese summer at the undulating Portimão circuit with the Championship fights well and truly alive in all three categories. Jonathan Rea extended his lead in World Superbike after another double win but it was the gutsy and heroic comeback races from Álvaro Bautista, coupled with the closest race finish of the season, that saw the fight for the 2019 World Championship crown re-ignited following an epic twenty-lap race on Sunday.

WorldSBK Race 1

It was the gentleman's set for Jonathan Rea who, after starting from pole position, obliterated the lap record in Portimão as he cruised to his 81st career win, more than three seconds ahead of Chaz Davies whose form from Laguna Seca continued in the opening race of the weekend.

Never headed, Rea was unstoppable, opening up a commanding 1.5s lead at the end of Lap 2.

Most of the action, however, came moments into the race. Álvaro Bautista, who was riding still not 100% fit following his triple DNF in the United States, was almost on the floor again at Turn 1. Teammate Davies, who had not made the best of his qualifying tyre, made arguably the best start of his WorldSBK career and out-braked eight riders into the opening right-hand corner. Davies' appearance alongside his teammate spooked the Spaniard, who sat up and collided with the rear end of Alex Lowes' Yamaha before running wide and re-joining at the back of the field.

As the race progressed the podium places seemed settled - Rea, Davies and Michael van der Mark, who rode sensibly to third after starting tenth on the grid. Bautista recovered to finish fourth after some precise overtakes, his late race pace as fast as Rea; had it not been for his Lap 1 skirmish, he may well have challenged the four-time Champion for the win. Leon Haslam took fifth after a race-long fight with Toprak Razgatlioglu who, like Davies, charged through the field after a poor qualifying session.

Race 1

1	Jonathan Rea	20 laps
2	Chaz Davies	+3.891s
3	Michael van der Mark	+6.168s

Tissot Superpole Race

1	Jonathan Rea	10 laps
2	Álvaro Bautista	+2.103s
3	Alex Lowes	+2.384s

Race 2

1	Álvaro Bautista	20 laps
2	Jonathan Rea	+0.111s
3	Toprak Razgatlioglu	+4.576s

SUPERSPORT
FIM WORLD CHAMPIONSHIP

1	Federico Caricasulo	13 laps (Red Flag)
2	Randy Krummenacher	+0.333s
3	Lucas Mahias	+0.645s

SUPERSPORT300
FIM WORLD CHAMPIONSHIP

1	Scott Deroue	11 laps
2	Manuel González	+0.153s
3	Ana Carrasco	+2.850s

Tissot Superpole Race

Jonathan Rea won his ninth race at Portimão on Sunday morning, once again leading from lights to flag after another convincing display aboard his Kawasaki. Pulling away by more than three tenths of a second a lap in the first half of the race, as we have seen so often, enabled the four-time Champion to control things at the front, crossing the line at the end of the ten-lap Tissot Superpole Race to notch up his 82nd career win by 2.103s.

Álvaro Bautista clawed his way back onto the podium after another steady opening lap saw him drop to ninth, the #19 clearly playing it safe after Saturday's Turn 1 collision. Matching Rea's pace, the Ducati star showed he was not prepared to go down without a fight, making some decisive moves on his rivals.

Bautista made easy work of overhauling Sandro Cortese and Toprak Razgatlioglu before using the power of his Panigale V4 R to pass Leon Haslam on Lap 5 and Tom Sykes a lap later.

Alex Lowes had made changes to his Yamaha overnight and had also moved forward relatively easily. The British rider, who was locked in a battle of teammates for third overall in the Championship standings, was displaying the kind of pace he had shown early in the season. Giving chase to runaway race leader Rea, P2 had been looking good until the charging Bautista unleashed a couple of blistering laps to lock onto his target. Within striking distance on Lap 8, Lowes responded immediately before Álvaro made the move stick on the penultimate lap after the pair crossed the line together.

Ducati power prevailed meaning it was Rea, Bautista and Lowes on the podium, the trio 1.7s ahead of Toprak Razgatlioglu who finished fourth after winning his own private battle with Leon Haslam. Michael van der Mark could only manage sixth. Tom Sykes salvaged seventh, a mere second ahead of Sandro Cortese, the German fending off Loris Baz who himself overhauled Chaz Davies for P9.

WorldSBK Race 2

After the drama in the opening races, Race 2 was simply spectacular with the top six riders covered by just over a second for the opening half dozen laps.

Rea once again made the most of his pole position start, hitting the front at Turn 1 from a highly motivated Toprak Razgatlioglu and Leon Haslam who made it a potential all-Kawasaki podium for the first four laps. With the leading group bunched together, all eyes were on Álvaro Bautista who, unlike in the previous two races, had made a much better start and was in the mix from the off. Moving into third on Lap 5, the WorldSBK rookie hit the front on Lap 6 and looked to have the race in his pocket.

A determined Rea dropped back to third after being passed by Razgatlioglu who pulled off an outstanding double overtake on both Bautista and Rea only to relinquish his brief lead to the Spanish rider almost immediately.

Toprak was classified sixth, the Turkish rider three seconds clear of Alex Lowes and more than ten seconds ahead of Sandro Cortese in eighth. Marco Melandri was able to fend off compatriot Michael Ruben Rinaldi for ninth, just missing out on P8 after a multi-lap battle with his teammate Cortese.

Tom Sykes was left scratching his head after finishing down in thirteenth after a Lap 7 crash. He had once again qualified strongly, putting the BMW S 1000 RR on the front row of the grid (second position), but struggled to convert his one lap pace as the track temperatures soared above 45 degrees.

Takumi Takahashi, fresh from a podium finish in the Suzuka 8 Hour race in Japan, was drafted in to replace Leon Camier at Honda. The Japanese rider, who made his WorldSBK debut in Portugal in 2017, claimed the final World Championship point in fifteenth.

As the race settled down, the top three began to ease away from the field but Rea was in race mode and, with Bautista's lead never more than 1.3s, the #1 applied the pressure. Álvaro was clearly on the limit, almost losing the front several times as he battled not just a loss of grip but the pain from his injured shoulder from Laguna Seca. As the last lap began, the gap was 0.8s with Jonathan producing a prodigeous last lap to almost snatch the win at the line.

But it would be Bautista who won, his fifteenth win of the season, and ensured that title fight was still well and truly alive, although the odds were very much in favour of Kawasaki-mounted Rea.

Razgatlioglu notched up an eighth podium of the year and his third top Independent win of the weekend. The talented Turk had opened up a comfortable gap of almost four seconds to the squabbling group behind.

Good friends off-track but rivals on it, Alex Lowes eventually got the better of Leon Haslam to take fourth. The duo fought tooth and nail throughout, with the #22 and #91 passing each other several times a lap in the final five alone. Loris Baz had late-race pace to finish sixth after he, like the two riders ahead of him, had to contend with the attentions Michael van der Mark who was in no mood to be beaten by the Frenchman.

Marco Melandri, Tom Sykes and Sandro Cortese completed the top ten ahead of Jordi Torres, Michael Ruben Rinaldi, Markus Reiterberger, Eugene Laverty and Leandro Mercado, who rounded out the points-scorers.

It was a day to forget for Chaz Davies who failed to score any points once again. A set-up change, that didn't work, was compounded by a technical problem with his gear lever. He could only manage P16, yet left the circuit happy enough following his Saturday podium.

WorldSSP

The Supersport World Championship was literally blown wide open in Portugal after a red flag cut short the eighteen-lap race. The cause of the stoppage was oil on the track courtesy of Raffaele De Rosa's MV Agusta engine failure – and this handed the win to Federico Caricasulo who had passed teammate and rival Randy Krummenacher just seconds earlier. A quick thinking De Rosa, who had saved a potential monster highside a lap

earlier, reacted quickly by alerting the marshals to the problem and preventing any further issues for him or the rest of the field still racing.

Krummenacher went into the weekend fifteen points ahead of his Yamaha teammate and was understandably unhappy with the outcome. The Swiss rider rode through the pain barrier following a Friday highside that saw him lucky to walk away without serious injury. Seemingly content to take it easy in the opening laps, Krummenacher eased past early pace-setters Isaac Viñales and Lucas Mahias, who once again were in the front-running fight from the start, before giving chase to his closest title challenger.

The rules state that, in the event of a red flag, the results are declared based on the last completed sector for each rider, extremely unlucky for the #21 who had relinquished the lead by a mere 0.333s at the aforementioned timing marker.

Lucas Mahias, who had taken podiums at Misano and Donington Park, made it three on the bounce, the 2017 World Champion and last year's runner-up showing incredible corner speed as he fought valiantly to stay with the two leading title contenders. Mahias was classified third ahead of Jules Cluzel who, despite pace early on, had no answer as the race progressed and was forced to back off significantly after being covered in oil from De Rosa's failing motorcycle ahead.

Viñales was having one of the best weekends of his short WorldSSP career until he went out with a technical problem. Running strongly at the front, the Spaniard appeared much more confident until his bike gave up the ghost: a third consecutive failure to score for the Supersport rookie.

Behind the leading quartet, Ayrton Badovini rode a consistent race to P5 as the one-time WorldSSP race winner (Sepang 2016) achieved his best result of the year. Corentin Perolari was impressive in sixth after fending off a quintet of riders. Hikari Okubo maintained fifth in the Championship after digging deep to claim seventh at the flag just ahead of Jules Danilo, who raced to his best WorldSSP result in eighth; the Frenchman narrowly beat a rejuvenated Loris Cresson and Miguel Pons, who showed his potential throughout the weekend to finish tenth as a wildcard at the event.

Gabriele Ruiu was drafted in on Friday evening to replace the injured Hannes Soomer, the Italian taking a well-earned eleventh ahead of former

WorldSSP300 race winner Dani Valle, who took twelfth on his WorldSSP debut.

WorldSSP300

Spain's Manuel González took another step closer to the World Championship after another scintillating performance in both Tissot Superpole and the race.

Starting from pole position, González once again put himself into podium contention early on before he was pushed back into the now usual packed front-running group.

With the usual multi-lap overtakes involving more than a dozen riders, it was Scott Deroue who made the break with only González able to go with him.

Behind the pair who were now clear of the chasing pack, it was all action behind, with Andy Verdoïa, Ana Carrasco, Marc García and in the early laps' half a dozen others all in the mix.

A jump-start for Bruno Ieraci removed him from the fight for the podium, whilst Beatriz Neila produced the race of her young career by running confidently in the lead group throughout.

Deroue and González swapped places several times in the closing stages but, at the flag, it was the Dutchman who took the win to keep his Championship hopes alive. González finished second, his fifth podium of the season, to set up a potential title-winning race in France. He would need only thirteen points there.

Ana Carrasco completed the podium at the circuit she made history at in 2017 to keep her slim hopes of retaining her crown a possibility.

García was clearly frustrated after being unable to slipstream Carrasco to the line, whilst Verdoïa and Nick Kalinin completed the top six. Neila rounded out her best on-track weekend in seventh ahead of Galang Hendra Pratama, Donington Park winner Kevin Sabatucci and Victor Steeman, who started on the front row but could only finish tenth in the race.

◀◀◀ *Circuit de Nevers Magny-Cours*
27 - 29 September

Un week-end magnifique for Toprak at Magny-Cours

The now customary final European race of the season took place at Magny-Cours with several titles up for grabs. With weather always a factor there was drama aplenty from the opening Free Practice sessions with both Álvaro Bautista and Champion elect Jonathan Rea hitting the deck early on. Thankfully both were unhurt, and the title fight resumed in earnest.

WorldSBK Race 1

Race 1, the 800th since WorldSBK began in 1988, didn't disappoint and was arguably the best race of the season. The combination of a mixed-up grid courtesy of inclement weather during Superpole, and the no holds barred on track shenanigans from lights out to the flag reminded everyone of why World Superbike racing is so popular.

Starting from pole, Champion elect Rea took the hole shot before Michael van der Mark leant on him into the Adelaide Hairpin, the pair banging fairings on the brakes and at the apex of the corner. It was a sign of what was to come as a leading group of seven swapped paint several times a lap for the first third of the race.

Starting from fourteenth and sixteenth on the grid respectively, Chaz Davies and Toprak Razgatlioglu sliced through the pack like a hot knife through butter, putting themselves into contention within the opening two laps. Chaz's time at the front was short lived - his Ducati suffered a technical glitch which caused him to crash at the end of Lap 3. Toprak was lucky not to go down with him as the pair collided just prior to the demise of the #7.

After leading for the first half dozen laps, Tom Sykes was passed by Michael van der Mark who looked as though he had the race win in the bag after opening up a 1.2s over Jonathan Rea, who also slipped ahead of Sykes on Lap 8. With Rea relentless in his pursuit of the Dutchman, the #60 made a 'silly mistake' crashing out on Lap 19, leaving the four-time Champion in the driving seat.

With a lap to go Jonathan Rea proved he is human after all, relinquishing a lead of over a second to allow Toprak Razgatlioglu to close to within striking distance with half a lap to go. Toprak was precision perfect, surprising Rea with a cheeky overtake on

PIRELLI FRENCH ROUND

SBK MOTUL
FIM SUPERBIKE WORLD CHAMPIONSHIP

Race 1

1	**Toprak Razgatlioglu**	21 laps
2	**Jonathan Rea**	+0.240s
3	**Tom Sykes**	+6.839s

Tissot Superpole Race

1	**Toprak Razgatlioglu**	10 laps
2	**Jonathan Rea**	+0.319s
3	**Michael van der Mark**	+1.486s

Race 2

1	**Jonathan Rea**	21 laps
2	**Michael van der Mark**	+0.862s
3	**Alex Lowes**	+1.702s

SUPERSPORT
FIM WORLD CHAMPIONSHIP

1	**Lucas Mahias**	12 laps
2	**Isaac Viñales**	+0.264s
3	**Ayrton Badovini**	+1.050s

SUPERSPORT300
FIM WORLD CHAMPIONSHIP

1	**Ana Carrasco**	12 laps
2	**Manuel González**	+0.233s
3	**Scott Deroue**	+0.430s

the brakes after the Imola chicane to win his first World Superbike race and thus becoming the first Turkish rider to do so. Rea was openly annoyed with himself for 'backing off too much' but on the other hand knew he had put a fifth world title within reach. It was a similar story for the final spot on the podium. Like Razgatlioglu, Sykes showed late race pace too, overhauling long time third place man Loris Baz to put his BMW onto the podium for the fourth time in 2019. Baz took another P4 with the accolade of being top Yamaha.

Álvaro Bautista salvaged fifth after a damage limitation race saw him post some impressive lap times on his debut race at the French track. Alex Lowes had a lonely final part to the race finishing sixth, six seconds behind Bautista and five seconds ahead of a returning Leon Camier, who gave Honda their best result of the season in seventh. Marco Melandri crossed the line in eighth after getting the better of the duelling Eugene Laverty and Sandro Cortese who were separated by less than a second at the flag. Jordi Torres came from the back of the grid to take eleventh ahead of Leandro Mercado, a remounted Michael van der Mark, Michael Ruben Rinaldi and Alessandro Delbianco, who took the final World Championship point.

Tissot Superpole Race
Sunday's opening race served up another treat with Saturday's winner Toprak Razgatlioglu keen to show that he could win on sheer pace alone.

With Rea fully aware that his finishing position in the Tissot Superpole Race would determine whether he could mathematically secure a fifth World title, he was on fire from the off, overtaking initial leader Michael van der Mark to hit the front on Lap 2, conscious that an attack from Toprak would come, he wasn't wrong.

The Turkish rider - who once again was buried in sixteenth on the grid - made up eight places on the opening lap, gaining three more on Lap 2 before overhauling VDM on Lap 5 in his pursuit of Rea. His pace was insane and thanks to a new outright circuit record on Lap 2 followed by several inch-perfect consistent laps, the

#54 overtook rival Rea with four laps to go. Rea gave it his all but, in the end, Razgatlioglu was just too good, crossing the line 0.3s ahead to make it a Magny-Cours double. The nine points achieved for Rea meant the title could be won in Race 2 but only if Álvaro Bautista failed to finish and the four-time Champion was victorious. Early pace setter Michael van der Mark clung on the final podium spot ahead of Ducati duo Chaz Davies and Álvaro Bautista.

Alex Lowes finished sixth ahead of Loris Baz and Tom Sykes, who was unable to replicate his Race 1 pace. Leon Haslam, who crashed out the battle for sixth on Saturday, took the final point in ninth.

WorldSBK Race 2
With so much drama and excitement in the opening two races nobody could have expected the outcome of Race 2, not even Jonathan Rea who re-wrote the record books again.

As in the Tissot Superpole Race it was Michael van der Mark who made the early running, leading from the start. Rea slotted into second with Álvaro Bautista running third at the end of the opening lap. Toprak Razgatlioglu was in the mix immediately thanks to his front row start but his aspirations of making it a treble win were over three minutes after the start. Losing the front at Chateau d'eau, Toprak hit the deck and took with him a luckless Bautista who had nowhere to go. Unable to restart, the Spanish rider's hopes of winning the World title now lay in the hands of Yamaha riders van der Mark and Alex Lowes who latched on to Rea who had in-turn taken the lead on Lap 6. Several changes of lead over the next couple of laps didn't slow the leading trio and with VDM back in front on Lap 8 the tension was palpable.

Rea, who by his own admission had not expected to take the title in France, knew that the win would be enough and after retaking the lead on Lap 11 he opened up a lead of a second to win his 83rd race in WorldSBK and an unprecedented fifth consecutive World Superbike Championship.

Yamaha celebrated a double podium with both van der Mark and Lowes, the pair a couple of seconds ahead of Chaz Davies who passed Loris Baz for fourth with a handful of laps to go. Marco Melandri finished a credible sixth on his final European appearance after edging Leon Haslam and Tom Sykes after a race-long fight with the Englishmen. Leon Camier was again in the top ten as was Jordi Torres.

Double STK1000 Champion Sylvain Barrier gave his new Ducati squad their first ever WorldSBK points in thirteenth.

WorldSSP

Lucas Mahias won an electrifying race in front of his home crowd after fending off Isaac Viñales on the final lap of a shortened twelve lap WorldSSP race.

Mahias, who started from fifth on the grid, was at the sharp end of the initial race start which was stopped on the opening lap following an incident involving Nacho Calero, Maximilian Bau and Federico Fuligni. When racing resumed it was Ayrton Badovini who hit the front after starting from third.

Four-time race winner at Magny-Cours Jules Cluzel took the lead after a couple of corners before the Championship was blown wide open after a monster highside for Randy Krummenacher who crashed out halfway around the opening lap. The action at the front was frantic but the drama had only just begun. Federico Caricasulo, who started the day second in the Championship behind teammate Krummenacher, eased into the lead on Lap 2, quickly opening up a lead of almost two seconds. With what looked like a potential fifteen-point lead heading the Italian's way he took slid out of contention. Desperate to salvage what points he could, the #64 remounted only to crash again two laps later leaving the top of the overall Championship standings the way they were before the WorldSSP protagonists arrived in France.

Cluzel did his best to cling on to the lead but it was evident he was lacking a little in terms of outright pace. He was slowly sucked back into the pack of seven that was now fighting for the three places on the podium.

Isaac Viñales, who was having his best race since the Thai round, took the lead briefly, as did Badovini before former World Champion Lucas Mahias made his bid for glory as the race passed two-thirds distance.

With two laps to go, Viñales had worked his way back into the lead and as the final lap began it was two-horse race - Viñales vs. Mahias. Mahias made his move, a carbon copy of the move made by Toprak Razgatlioglu to win Saturday's Superbike opener, four corners from home to become the first non-Yamaha win in two years. Viñales was delighted with his first World Supersport podium, whilst Ayrton Badovini was rejuvenated in third after returning to the podium for the first time since Sepang 2016.

Raffaele De Rosa eventually clawed his way to fourth at the flag ahead of Hikari Okubo, whilst Cluzel eventually finished sixth to keep his brief hopes of the WorldSSP title alive. The Frenchman finished just over a second ahead of teammate Corentin Perolari who could may well have been in the fight for the podium if he hadn't had to take avoiding action following Krummenacher's Lap 1 exit. Thomas Gradinger was back in action after missing Portimão through injury and he took a solid eighth.

Kyle Smith, who started from pole position for the first time in his career, finished ninth to become the 2019 FIM Europe Supersport Cup Winner. The British rider was able to hold off a late surge by Peter Sebestyen, who completed the top ten.

Christian Stange scored his first World Championship points of the season in thirteenth whilst Xavier Navand scored the first WorldSSP point of his young career after finishing fifteenth.

WorldSSP300

Manuel González became the youngest ever FIM Motorcycle Road Racing Champion after finishing second in another closely fought WorldSSP300 race, beating the previous record set by Loris Capirossi in the 125cc World Championship in 1990 by 109 days.

González appeared to be on the back foot as the weekend began, qualifying fifteenth whilst his main title rivals where all in the top four.

When the lights went out though it was business as usual for the seventeen-year-old who sliced his way through the field and into the leading quartet by the end of the second lap, hitting the front on Lap 4.

Passes aplenty enabled Ana Carrasco to open a gap of a second which she soon relinquished as the pack behind set a blistering pace in their pursuit of the reigning Champion.

Scott Deroue made his bid for glory on the final lap only to see it taken away immediately by Carrasco, who hung on to win at the venue that saw crowned the first female road racing World Champion twelve months ago. Deroue was forced to settle for third as González, who had seemingly been content to sit in fourth passed both Andy Verdoïa and the Dutchman on the final lap. Verdoïa had to be content with fourth after putting up a valiant effort to win for the first time in front of his home crowd.

Behind the top four Galang Hendra Pratama held on to fifth after an epic ride from twenty-ninth on the grid for Livio Loi saw him claim his best result since joining the WorldSSP300 grid in sixth.

Bruno Ieraci, Jeffrey Buis, Victor Steeman and Nick Kalinin completed the top ten.

◀◀◀ *Circuito San Juan Villicum* *11 - 13 October*

Apexes aced in Argentina for Jonathan and Álvaro

MOTUL ARGENTINEAN ROUND

The second ever WorldSBK event at the San Juan Villicum Circuit provided some excellent racing, as it had in 2018, but it wasn't without drama before the lights went out for Race 1. A slippery track surface and fluctuating temperatures from the opening Free Practice sessions meant the circuit was unpredictable, with some riders demanding that racing be postponed. The end result was six riders sitting out Race 1, which went ahead without incident. All riders took the grid for the remaining races.

WorldSBK Race 1

Álvaro Bautista took his 16th win of the year on his first visit to the San Juan Villicum Circuit. As the pit lane opened half a dozen riders, Chaz Davies, Eugene Laverty, Ryuichi Kiyonari, Sandro Cortese, Marco Melandri and Leon Camier, made the decision to not participate in the opening twenty-one lap encounter, leaving just twelve bikes on the grid.

Starting from pole, Álvaro Bautista came under immediate attack from newly crowned and now five-time Superbike World Champion Jonathan Rea, and regular front runners Michael van der Mark and Toprak Razgatlioglu who for the opening few laps were evenly matched. A few lively moments almost saw the leading two on the floor, but their pace was consistent and although clearly struggling for grip, they were able to break the front running pack with only Razgatlioglu able to follow.

Rea gave it everything, his Kawasaki looking every bit the match for the Ducati, but despite a couple of brief spells out front, the #1 had to be content with second place. Bautista set several fastest laps to eventually take the win by 1.5s at the flag.

Razgatlioglu, still brimming with confidence after a stunning double win in France a fortnight ago, finished on the podium for the eleventh time in 2019, replicating his Race 1 result at the Argentine venue from twelve months ago. Michael van der Mark kept his hopes of finishing third overall in the final standings alive with a solid fourth place finish after starting from second on

CIRCUITO SAN JUAN VILLICUM

Race 1

1	**Toprak Razgatlioglu**	21 laps
2	**Jonathan Rea**	+0.240s
3	**Tom Sykes**	+6.839s

Tissot Superpole Race

1	**Toprak Razgatlioglu**	10 laps
2	**Jonathan Rea**	+0.319s
3	**Michael van der Mark**	+1.486s

Race 2

1	**Jonathan Rea**	21 laps
2	**Michael van der Mark**	+0.862s
3	**Alex Lowes**	+1.702s

SUPERSPORT FIM WORLD CHAMPIONSHIP

1	**Lucas Mahias**	12 laps
2	**Isaac Viñales**	+0.264s
3	**Ayrton Badovini**	+1.050s

the grid, the former WorldSSP Champion eventually finished thirteen seconds away from the podium.

Despite every effort to stay with the leading group, Alex Lowes gradually dropped back into the clutches of Leon Haslam who, no matter how hard he tried, was unable to pass his British counterpart. The pair finished fifth and sixth respectively, comfortably ahead of Tom Sykes who overcame a couple of technical problems earlier in the weekend to bag nine valuable World Championship points in seventh.

Jordi Torres rode a sensible race after being in two minds about taking to the grid, he finished almost ten seconds behind Sykes in eighth. Local hero Leandro Mercado came from the back of the grid to salvage ninth ahead of WorldSBK rookie Alessandro Delbianco. A superb qualifying session saw Alessandro Delbianco eighth on the grid with pace that he was able to replicate in race conditions. After running a strong seventh in the early laps he took tenth at the flag. Markus Reiterberger and Michael Ruben Rinaldi were the only other riders to be classified in eleventh and twelfth positions respectively.

Tissot Superpole Race

After Saturday's depleted grid, it was business as usual in the Tissot Superpole Race and business as usual for Jonathan Rea who claimed his third win at the San Juan Villicum circuit. In what was a pretty dominant ten lap dash, Rea smashed the lap record by a staggering 1.7s to take the flag a comfortable 2.1s ahead of Álvaro Bautista, who gave it everything in his pursuit of the five-time WorldSBK Champion. Toprak Razgatlioglu was the final rider to stand on the podium after taking his twelfth podium of the year, the Turkish rider putting in another strong race to finish a second and a half behind the #19 rider.

After electing not to race a day earlier, Chaz Davies took fourth, despite a poor start that saw him seventh at the end of the opening lap. Alex Lowes finished ahead of Michael van der Mark by over a second, the #60 finishing two seconds ahead of Sandro Cortese. Cortese was in-turn four seconds clear of Leon Haslam, who by his own admission, was having a weekend to forget. Tom Sykes salvaged eighth for the BMW Motorrad squad, the 2013 World Champion having to work hard to keep Leandro Mercado at bay.

WorldSBK Race 2

After taking his 70th career win twelve months ago,

Jonathan Rea took his 70th win for Kawasaki in Sunday's second twenty-one lap race at the Circuito San Juan Villicum, crossing the line five seconds clear of Chaz Davies who was back on the podium for the eighth time this year. Toprak Razgatlioglu took a third consecutive podium of the weekend, to clinch the 2019 top Independent rider's crown, after another solid ride saw him move to within six points of third overall in the points classification. The Turkish rider dropped to fourth on Lap 9 before retaking third on Lap 13 but was unable to stay with the leading two riders.

Michael van der Mark closed to within one point of Alex Lowes after finishing fourth. The Dutchman was able to overhaul early front runner Álvaro Bautista on Lap 17 of the twenty-one after the Spanish rider, who finished fifth, suffered a mid-race drop in pace. Alex Lowes finished sixth, a position he took from Sandro Cortese on Lap 8.

Local hero Leandro 'Tati' Mercado rode arguably the best race of his World Superbike career, slicing his way through the field from dead last on the grid to eighth. The #36 rider got the better of Jordi Torres and Leon Haslam who completed the top ten and finished a few bike lengths behind Eugene Laverty, who also produced the goods when it mattered, finishing seventh after ending Lap 1 a lowly seventeenth.

After showing a stunning pace on Friday, Michael Ruben Rinaldi was only able to finish eleventh, losing pace once again as the race progressed following a lack of adhesion from the soft rear tyre that he chose. The Italian finished just over half-a-second ahead of a battered Loris Baz who rode through the pain barrier, following two massive highsides to finish twelfth. Leon Camier finished a lonely thirteenth, comfortably ahead of Yamaha teammates Marco Melandri and Sandro Cortese, the German left bemused after a significant loss of grip saw him plummeting back through the pack after running a strong fourth for the opening couple of laps.

WorldSSP
The WorldSSP title would be decided in Qatar with three possible victors after one of the most intense races in recent World Supersport memory.

Corentin Perolari made the most of his first ever World Supersport pole position to lead the first lap before relinquishing his early advantage to teammate Jules Cluzel, who had started from third place on the grid. The action at the front was frenetic with the leading group of seven riders locked together in usual WorldSSP fashion and with riders fighting for track position it was Cluzel, the winner in Argentina in 2018,

who made the decision to try to escape. It was a gamble that paid off, the Frenchman eased away by more than half a second a lap to take his third win of the year by 2.4s.

Lucas Mahias' recent run of form on the Kawasaki continued in Argentina, the former World Champion clearly now at home with the Italian Puccetti team and the Japanese manufacturer. He finished second to record his fifth consecutive podium finish, guaranteeing a fourth place overall in the final points standing whatever happens in Qatar.

Isaac Viñales took his second consecutive WorldSSP podium after being in the right place at the right time. Having been in the leading group, albeit at the back of it, the Spanish rider seized the opportunity when it presented itself. Federico Caricasulo has openly said he will do what it takes to win the title and he clearly meant it after the Italian's attempt to pass Championship leader Randy Krummenacher sent the pair wide a couple of laps from home, allowing Raffaele De Rosa to simply hold his line and pass the pair of them. Perolari was able to hang on to fourth by 0.068s from Caricasulo who tried everything he could to make amends for his earlier misdemeanour.

The #3 of De Rosa was classified sixth ahead of Randy Krummenacher who finished seventh and saw his Championship lead cut to a mere eight points after his worst finish of the year. The Swiss rider, who has led the Championship since the opening round in Australia, launched a scathing post-race attack on his team, insinuating they had not given him an engine on par with teammate and main title rival Caricasulo's. This was rebuffed by the team who said that it was not in their interest to slow or hamper either rider given that both could potentially deliver them the crown.

Thomas Gradinger, Kyle Smith and Ayrton Badovini lost touch with the leading seven around half race distance, the trio having lonely races for the final 50% of the nineteen-lap race. Peter Sebestyen, Hikari Okubo, Christian Stange, Loris Cresson and Hannes Soomer were the final points scorers.

Next up, the season finale, where the Championship would be sorted out one way or another.

Losail Internacional Circuit
24 - 26 October

Rea dances to a triple in the desert

Round thirteen of the Motul FIM Superbike World Championship gave fans trackside and around the world five great races, a fitting floodlit finale for a sensational year of racing. Jonathan Rea took another triple in WorldSBK - there was tension throughout the fifteen lap WorldSSP race and a photo finish decided the first ever WorldSSP300 race to be held in Qatar and indeed outside of Europe.

WorldSBK Race 1

Drama on the Warm Up lap saw Jordi Torres crash after water leaking from his Kawasaki soaked his rear tyre. Several riders took avoiding action and the race began without delay, with Torres returning to the pits unable to take part.

Jonathan Rea signalled his intentions for the weekend immediately, hitting the front from the off. Never headed and despite a valiant attempt to stay in contention by Alex Lowes, Rea took the win by almost three seconds, seemingly able to open the gap when it suited.

Lowes, who openly admits to enjoying racing under the floodlights in Qatar, rode arguably the race of his season, digging deep in the early stages to ensure he was clear of any mid-pack trouble. He eventually finished third after succumbing to Chaz Davies, who equally put in a performance that most would have been proud of. Twelfth on the grid to second at the flag, Davies was fourth at the end of Lap 1 and whilst unable to stay with Rea, the #7 was able to open a similar gap back to Lowes who took the final podium spot.

Álvaro Bautista went backwards at the start but recovered from ninth to finish fourth in what was a lonely race for the 2019 Championship runner-up.

Leon Haslam, a winner at the Losail International Circuit in 2015, took fifth in a photo finish with Michael van der Mark, a mere 0.018s splitting the pair after seventeen intense laps. Loris Baz watched it all unfold in front of hit; the Frenchman finished eighth with the accolade of being top Independent rider. Markus Reiterberger was the best BMW in ninth after Tom Sykes compromised his weekend after crashing out on Lap 2 - he had

MOTUL QATAR ROUND

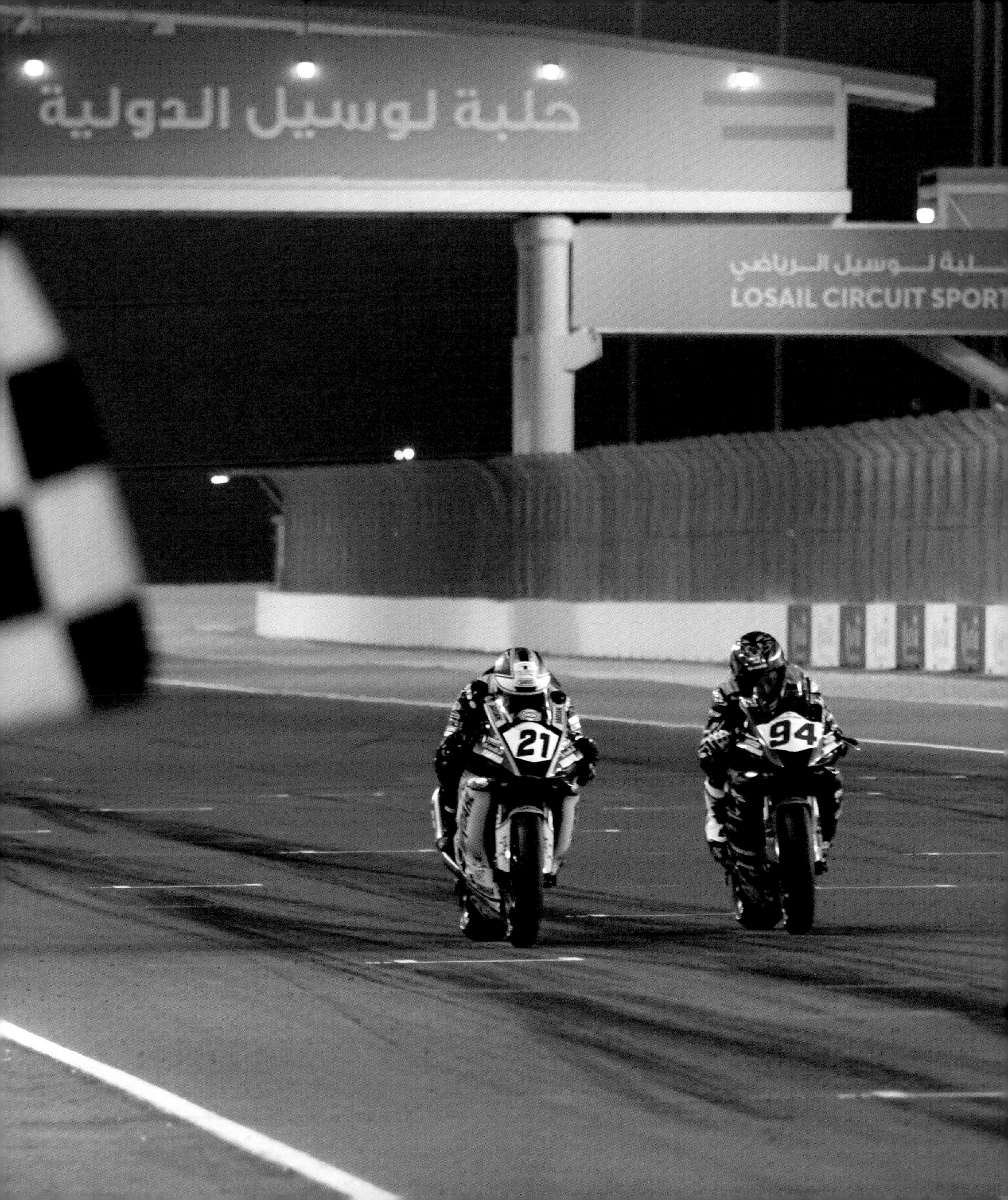
حلبة لوسيل الدولية
LOSAIL CIRCUIT SPORT
21
94

Race 1

1. **Jonathan Rea** — 17 laps
2. **Chaz Davies** — +2.732s
3. **Alex Lowes** — +5.423s

Tissot Superpole Race

1. **Jonathan Rea** — 10 laps
2. **Álvaro Bautista** — +2.027s
3. **Alex Lowes** — +5.143s

Race 2

1. **Jonathan Rea** — 17 laps
2. **Chaz Davies** — +2.978s
3. **Álvaro Bautista** — +3.100s

SUPERSPORT
FIM WORLD CHAMPIONSHIP

1. **Lucas Mahias** — 15 laps
2. **Jules Cluzel** — +0.868s
3. **Isaac Viñales** — +3.332s

SUPERSPORT300
FIM WORLD CHAMPIONSHIP

1. **Scott Deroue** — 10 laps
2. **Koen Meuffels** — +0.010s
3. **Bruno Ieraci** — +0.249s

qualified fourth. Eugene Laverty took another top ten finish in ninth ahead of Honda's Leon Camier, who said later that evening that he had 'got the best result possible'.

Toprak Razgatlioglu couldn't find his groove and after a series of mistakes and off-track moments he finished eleventh ahead of Marco Melandri (who was racing in his final World Superbike event), Michael Ruben Rinaldi, Ryuichi Kiyonari and Alessandro Delbianco, who took the final point on his Losail debut.

Tissot Superpole Race

After winning the manufacturers title on Friday evening, it was another easy Kawasaki win for Jonathan Rea on Saturday afternoon, who smashed the race lap record on his first flying lap, to win for the 87th time in WorldSBK by a commanding 2.027s at the flag.

Rea's pace in recent Tissot Superpole outings had been relentless and he once again controlled things from the front once clear of the field.

Alex Lowes made another strong start, running inside the top three throughout. The #22 had to be content with another P3 after losing out to the Ducati of Álvaro Bautista. The Spanish rider looked a lot more comfortable after reverting to a base setting for the shorter ten lap race. Lowes, in third, had to work hard to keep Leon Haslam behind him; the former Losail race winner finishing fourth after giving it his all in his final race for Kawasaki. Haslam finished a handful of bike lengths ahead of Chaz Davies, who despite moving through the field from row four, was unable to replicate his pace of the previous evening.

Behind the top five, Michael van der Mark edged out Loris Baz in an all Yamaha duel for sixth, with Sandro Cortese finishing eighth, less than a second behind the pair. Eugene Laverty took ninth to ensure a third row start for his final race with Ducati.

The fight for third overall in the final classification became a two-horse race following the Tissot Superpole Race after Toprak Razgatlioglu suffered a technical problem at the start and whilst the Turkish rider would make it back on track for the final race of the season, the bronze medal would go to either Yamaha-mounted Lowes or his teammate Michael van der Mark.

WorldSBK Race 2

Jonathan Rea was unstoppable once again in the final race of the season despite a spirited fight from Álvaro Bautista, who certainly showed no fear of attacking the five-time World Champion repeatedly in the opening half of the race.

Taking the lead from the start, Rea was unable to create an immediate gap over his pursuers like he had in the Tissot Superpole Race, finding himself on the receiving end of some hard but fair moves from the #19. Not phased in the slightest, Rea gave as good as he got, retaking the lead almost immediately

after every Ducati overtake. As it had been for most of the season, the battle was enthralling and neither rider was prepared to back down.

Chaz Davies, who worked his way up to third on Lap 4 after a series of fastest laps, made a bid for glory ten laps later, easing past teammate Bautista. Maintaining his pace, he was able to retain second but could do nothing about Rea, who took his second triple of the season at the flag.

Nine seconds adrift of the podium, Alex Lowes secured third overall in the World Championship after finishing a solid fourth to end his most successful season in WorldSBK with a top three overall. Toprak Razgatlioglu finished fifth to secure fifth in the Championship, the 2019 Independent Winner's result in the final race enough to guarantee Turkish Puccetti Racing the WorldSBK Independent Teams' Championship. Eugene Laverty showed incredible end-of-race pace to take sixth, equalling his season's best from MotorLand Aragón and reminding everyone that he too could well be in the mix next year when he moves to BMW.

Michael van der Mark and Loris Baz had another private battle for seventh, the Dutchman once again able to keep his Yamaha ahead of the #76. Baz in-turn rode brilliantly to recover from sixteenth at the end of Lap 1 after an off-track excursion at the start. Leon Haslam and Sandro Cortese finished ninth and tenth respectively, with Leandro Mercado, Tom Sykes, Jordi Torres, Markus Reiterberger and Michael Ruben Rinaldi taking the final points of the season.

Marco Melandri didn't have the fairy-tale swansong that he was hoping for but that didn't stop the former World Superbike runner-up from performing a huge burnout in Parc Ferme at the end of his final race. The Italian retires from motorcycle racing after an illustrious career saw him at the forefront of World Championship action for over two decades.

WorldSSP

The World Supersport Championship once again came down to the final race of the season, and with the top three protagonists taking the three places on the front row of the grid, the stage was set.

Multiple Championship runner-up in the past, Jules Cluzel, knew his only chance of winning the title was to win the race and the Frenchman made it into Turn 1 first, followed by his teammate Corentin Perolari who, as he had in Argentina two weeks earlier, played shotgun for his teammate for the opening handful of laps.

Federico Caricasulo failed to take advantage of his pole position, ending Lap 1 in fifth. His Championship-leading teammate, Randy Krummenacher, who had qualified second, made a much better getaway and ended Lap 1 in third.

With Cluzel maintaining a competitive pace, 2017 and 2018 Losail race winner Lucas Mahias slowly went about his business, moving into podium contention on Lap 2 before involving himself in a three-way scrap with Perolari and Isaac Viñales who had joined the party at the front by Lap 7.

With the top half-dozen riders tightly bunched, every position mattered and as the race moved towards half distance, provisionally, only seven points covered the top three title contenders.

Krummenacher, who had lost touch with the leading group, knew that all he had to do was follow his Italian rival Caricasulo to take the crown. As the leading four began to pull away, the Swiss rider was seemingly content to follow his teammate who was still circulating in fifth.

Back at the front, the battle continued to rage: Lucas Mahias hit the front on Lap 9 with Cluzel glued to rear of his compatriots' machine. Isaac Viñales worked hard to stay with the leading two but was unable to mount a serious challenge for the win. He did however edge ahead of the #16 to move into second, albeit briefly. The Spanish rider was nevertheless happy to claim a third consecutive podium behind Cluzel, who retook second after failing to counter Mahias' earlier attack. Mahias took the win, his third in succession at the Losail International Circuit, and the second in 2019 for Kawasaki by almost a second, signalling that he will be a contender for title glory in 2020.

Caricasulo finished fourth to get the better of Krummenacher in their own private battle, but it was the Swiss rider who won the war, clinching the WorldSSP title by six points. Corentin Perolari took a hard fought sixth after playing the team game throughout. He came home ahead of Raffaele De Rosa and Hikari Okubo who closed in rapidly on the battle for fourth towards the end. Kyle Smith and Ayrton Badovini rounded out the top ten ahead of Peter Sebestyen. Thomas Gradinger, who battled a severe fever all weekend, finished his race in twelfth ahead of Jules Danilo, Hannes Soomer and Glenn van Straalen, who was back in the points for the first time since Assen.

WorldSSP 300

Ana Carrasco made history once again by taking the first ever WorldSSP300 pole position in Qatar, the 2018 World Champion showing incredible pace around the 5.3km circuit. In the mix throughout the weekend, the outgoing Champion knew that a race win the following evening would give her the runner-up spot in this year's standings, but this is World Supersport 300 and anything can happen.

From lights out to the flag, a leading group of eight riders were never separated by more than two seconds. With the pack swapping positions sometimes two or three times a corner, let alone a lap, the on-track action was frantic.

Racing hard but fair, Carrasco fought back after being pushed wide early on, repaying the compliment to anyone that showed her a front wheel. Scott Deroue, also in the fight for the runner-up spot overall, ensured he was in contention, with a series of aggressive overtakes. Bruno Ieraci and Tom Edwards also battled hard, as both taken a first front row start of the year in Tissot Superpole. Koen Mueffels, the winner of the first round of the 2018 WorldSSP300 Championship at MotorLand Aragón, sliced through the pack, coming from sixteenth on the grid to third by the end of Lap 6.

As the ten-lap race neared its conclusion, it was clear that slipstreaming would play a huge part in the outcome of the final race of the season. The gap was so small that as the pack crossed the line a photo finish was declared. After a few minutes, the official review announced Scott Deroue as the winner. The Dutchman took the win by 0.010s from his teammate Mueffels, in the closest race in the history of the Championship.

A fraction behind, Bruno Ieraci took a career first World Championship podium after winning his own slipstream battle against newly-crowned World Champion Manuel González, who ended his season with fourth after once again being in the hunt for the win. Ana Carrasco was shuffled back to fifth ahead of Tom Edwards, who survived a heart stopping out of the seat moment through the fast Turn 7 – Turn 9 sequence of corners with two laps to go.

Galang Hendra Pratama inherited seventh after Marc García crashed out on the final lap; the Indonesian rider was part of the leading group throughout but unable to make any real impression. Frenchman Andy Verdoïa finished a lonely eighth ahead of countryman Hugo de Cancellis, whilst Dutchman Dion Otten who completed the top ten. Unai Orradre, Jeffrey Buis, Samuel di Sora, Kevin Sabatucci and Nick Kalinin took the final points in eleventh to fifteenth positions respectively.

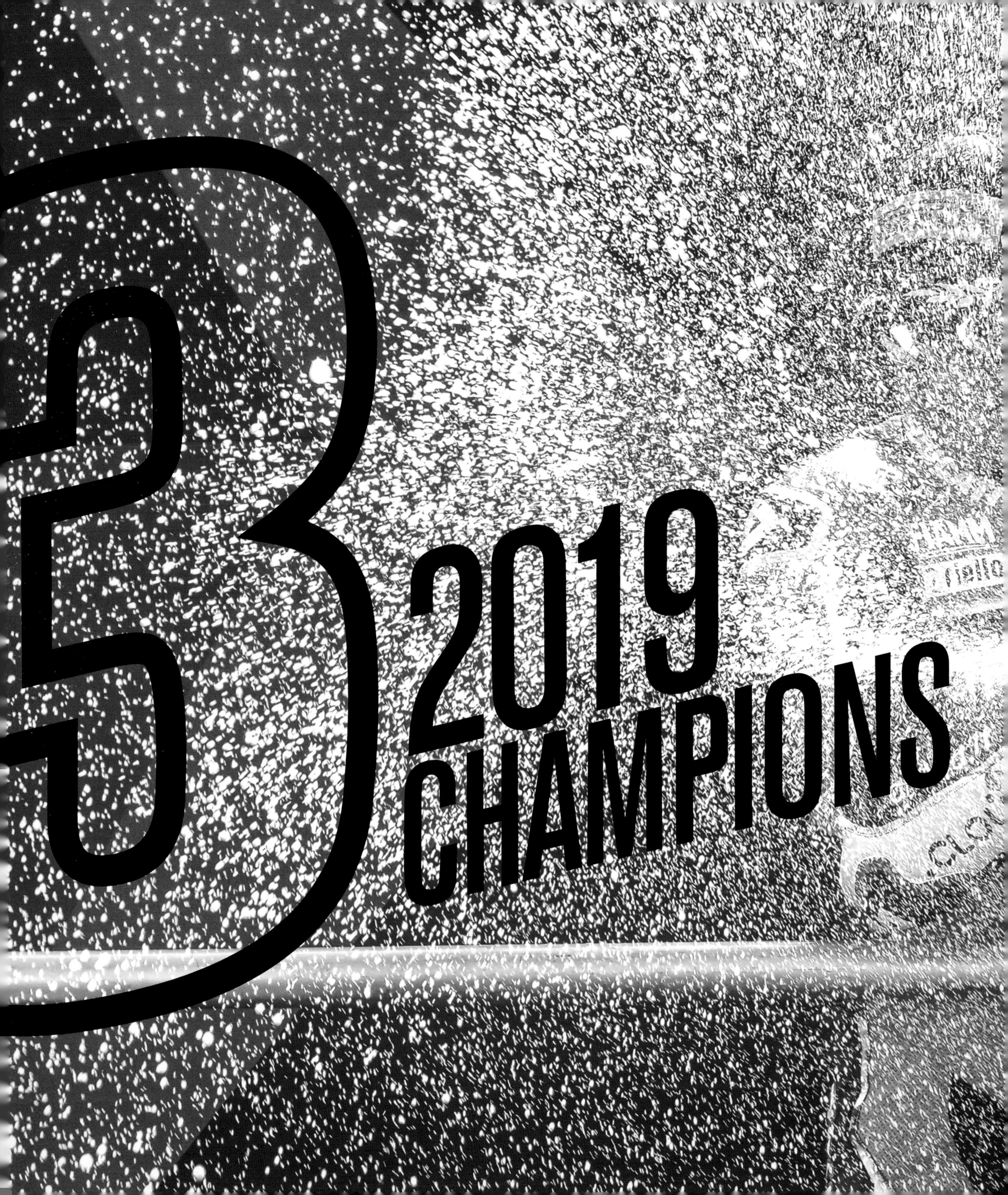
3
2019
CHAMPIONS

FIM SUPERBIKE WORLD CHAMPIONSHIP

Rea relentless as he seals fifth title

Eighty-eight individual race wins, more than seventy for Kawasaki and more than anyone in the history of the FIM Superbike World Championship, and a fifth consecutive WorldSBK crown, have cemented Jonathan Rea's name into the all-time greats of WorldSBK.

Progressing quickly through the smaller classes within the British Championship, Rea shot to prominence on the World stage in 2008, taking a maiden World Supersport race win at Brno on his way to the runner up spot in the title race.

After making his WorldSBK debut for Honda at the end of 2008, his first World Superbike win came in San Marino in 2009. Rea stayed loyal to HRC, and in 2012 they offered him MotoGP™ outings as a replacement for the then injured Casey Stoner. He finished a credible eighth and seventh respectively at the Misano World Circuit Marco Simoncelli and at MotorLand Aragón.

With Honda unable to provide an upgraded machine, Rea switched camps in 2015, joining Kawasaki and the World Championship winning KRT squad who were rewarded with instant success.

After his inaugural title, the #65 rider, as he was then, made it back to back Championship wins the following year to match the achievements of Fred Merkel, Doug Polen and Carl Fogarty. But Jonathan wasn't finished there. He went on to make it three on the bounce in 2017, the first rider in WorldSBK history to achieve the feat, before making it four in a row in 2018.

It was twelve races into his 2019 campaign before Rea would taste the Prosecco Doc for the first time in his strive to make it five. A determination to dig deep and a never give up attitude saw one of the largest pendulum swings in more than three decades of World Superbike competition as the #1 took an unprecedented fifth World Championship by 165 points as the final chequered flag was waved in Qatar.

With a year left on his current Kawasaki contract, Rea's motivation is his fear of losing and the Northern Irishman shows no sign of relinquishing the crown that he has worn unchallenged for the past five seasons. The 2019 season is over but the countdown to Phillip Island and the start of the 2020 campaign is on and if whilst there are many things unknown about the year ahead one thing is certain – Jonathan Rea WILL be in the mix for six.

2019
WORLD
CHAMPION

Krummenacher crowned King of WorldSSP in Qatar

A fifth-place finish in Qatar was enough for Randy Krummenacher to clinch the 2019 FIM Supersport World Championship crown, who became the first Swiss rider since Tom Luthi in 2005 (125cc) to win a World Championship title.

Krummenacher strung together a fantastic campaign, his third in WorldSSP, to take the number one spot by the narrowest of margins… six points.

The twenty-nine-year-old made his World Championship debut in 2006, in the 125cc category. He took his only podium in the class in 2007, at the Catalan GP.

A year later and it could have been the end of what has been a strong career for the likeable Swiss rider. A training crash on a snow-covered downhill run while mountain biking resulted in life saving surgery to remove his spleen. After initially being diagnosed with a bruised rib he attempted to ride at the Spanish Grand Prix in Jerez the following week. After falling ill at the circuit, he was taken to the local hospital, where it was revealed that he had lost three litres of blood.

After campaigning KTM machinery for three years he switched to Aprilia for the 2009 and 2010 125cc GP seasons before moving into Moto2 in 2011. Five years that yielded thirty-three-point scoring finishes including a best of fourth in Moto2 followed, before Krummenacher moved into the WorldSBK paddock, with Puccetti Racing for a debut season in World Supersport in 2016.

The transition to production-based machinery brought instant success, the #21 winning on his debut in Phillip Island, on his way to third overall in the final standings. He switched to World Superbike with the squad the following year achieving a best finish of seventh in Misano.

Back in Supersport for 2018, Randy was again at the forefront of the action, taking fourth overall twelve months ago. He romped to the title in 2019 after winning four races and achieving eight podium finishes out of the twelve races.

2019
WORLD
CHAMPION

Manuel González, Master of WorldSSP300

Manuel González not only became the third consecutive Spanish rider to win the FIM Supersport 300 World Championship, he became the youngest ever FIM solo motorcycle Road Racing Champion after wrapping up the 2019 title at the Circuit de Nevers Magny-Cours in France.

After switching the ParkinGO Kawasaki squad for the 2019 campaign, González had an almost perfect season. Three wins in the opening four races made him the one to beat, and despite his age, the racer from Madrid showed no sign of crumbling under the pressure as the title race heated up in Portugal. He ended the season 30 points ahead of his nearest rival with three wins and a total of six podium finishes from the nine races.

Manuel was involved with racing from an early age, regularly travelling to watch his father compete. He began riding bikes at the age of three, winning the Madrid Minibike Championship in 2010.

He won his first race on a Grand Prix Circuit (Jerez), in 2014 when competing in the Challenge 80cc Spanish Cup before progressing quickly through the ranks and joining the Red Bull Rookies grid in 2016 where he took a best result of 6th. He clinched the European Talent Cup with a winning margin of more than twenty points in 2017, before making his debut in WorldSSP300 as a wildcard at Jerez the same year. 6th overall on his first appearance as a full-time rider, he finished on the podium an impressive three times, taking third positions at Misano, Portimão and Magny-Cours.

A front runner throughout 2019, he will move directly into World Supersport for 2020.

2019 WORLD CHAMPION

RIDERS' RITUALS

Markus Reiterberger #28

Michael van der Mark #60

Eugene Laverty #50

Alex Lowes #22

Loris Baz #76

Jordi Torres #81

Michael Ruben Rinaldi #21

Leon Haslam #91

Chaz Davies #7

Michelle Pirro #51

Yuki Takahashi #72

Sandro Cortese #11

Jonathan Rea #1

Tom Sykes #66

123

Álvaro Bautista #19

Leandro Mercado #36

Toprak Razgatlioglu #54

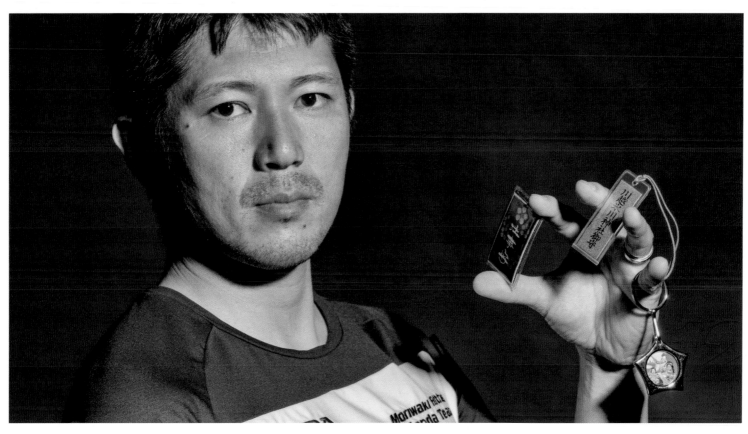

Ryuichi Kiyonari #23

5 FAIRINGS OFF

KAWASAKI

Kawasaki have been a dominant force in WorldSBK in recent years. World titles for Tom Sykes (2013), and five consecutive rider titles courtesy of Jonathan Rea (2015, 2016, 2017, 2018 and 2019), have propelled the Japanese manufacturer back to the forefront of the superbike market.

Part of the Superbike World Championship in various guises since it began, Kawasaki first won the WorldSBK crown in 1993 thanks to the efforts of American Scott Russell.

The green machines would have to wait for twenty years for their

*From the street to the track: **Kawasaki Ninja ZX-10RR***

x

128

Kawasaki bikes & teams   *42 Bikes, 23 Teams*

Kawasaki Racing Team WorldSBK
Turkish Puccetti Racing
Orelac Racing VerdNatura
Team Pedercini Racing

Kawasaki Puccetti Racing
Orelac Racing VerdNatura
Team Hartog - Against Cancer
EAB Racing Team
Team Pedercini Racing

Kawasaki Provec WorldSSP300
2R Racing Team
Nutec - RT Motorsports by SKM – Kawasaki
Prodina IRCOS Kawasaki
Kawasaki MOTOPORT
Kawasaki ParkinGO Team
Kawasaki GP Project
Scuderia Maranga Racing
DS Junior Team
Carl Cox-RT Motorsports by SKM-Kawasaki
Flembbo Leader Team
Turkish Puccetti Racing by TSM
MTM Racing Team
ACCR Czech Talent Team - Willi Race

second FIM Superbike World Championship crown, despite front-running performances following their 1993 triumph.

The Kawasaki ZX-10RR is at the pinnacle of modern-day Superbike technology, the Japanese manufacturer using WorldSBK both to develop technology for its road machine and showcase its strengths on track with a pure 'homologation special'.

The 'Ninja' will once again be the bike to beat as WorldSBK enters its 33rd year of competition in 2020.

In addition to racing in WorldSBK, Kawasaki was present on the grid in WorldSSP and WorldSSP300 in 2019. Podiums and wins aplenty in both categories, teenager Manuel González gave Kawasaki the FIM Supersport 300 World Championship title after a stunning season ,whilst Lucas Mahias took the first non-Yamaha win in two years in World Supersport, after winning in France, backing it up at the final round.

Kawasaki won both the WorldSBK and WorldSSP300 Manufacturer's titles in 2019.

KAWASAKI *ZX-10RR*

Fuel tank capacity
22 litres

Chassis
Cast aluminium

ENGINE

Type
1000cc 4 cylinder

Gearbox
Six speed

Maximum Power
+240 hp

Suspension
Showa through rodCast

Brakes
Brembo EVO

Weight
168 kg

DUCATI

Ducati remains the most successful manufacturer in World Superbike history.

In the hands of Marco Lucchinelli, the Ducati 851 went down in history as the first ever FIM Superbike World Championship event winner at Donington Park in 1988.

Their first riders' Championship came courtesy of Frenchman Raymond Roche, who triumphed in 1990.

Thirteen rider titles have followed, the last courtesy of Carlos Checa who won the 2011 edition of the series on the 1098R.

*From the street to the track: **Ducati Panigale V4 R***

Ducati bikes & teams   *4 Bikes, 3 Teams*

ARUBA.IT Racing Ducati
BARNI Racing Team
Team Goeleven

The 1199 Panigale R, which debuted in 2013, celebrated its maiden win at the Aragón Round in the hands of Chaz Davies in 2015 and went on to finish second in the overall standings in the hands of the Welshman in 2015, 2017 and 2018 as well as third overall in 2016.

Ducati changed its philosophy for 2019, ditching the 1199 Panigale R in favour of an all-new four-cylinder machine.

Despite Álvaro Bautista's sensational start to the 2019 season, no Championship titles have been delivered to the Bologna factory since Checa's impressive season. That said, Ducati continue to be front-runners and remain one of the most well-loved manufacturers within WorldSBK. With both factory riders winning races aboard their all-new Panigale V4 R in its debut season, all eyes will be on the final Championship standings at the end of 2020.

DUCATI *PANIGALE V4 R*

Fuel tank capacity
23.9 litres

Chassis
Aluminium front frame

ENGINE

Type
4-stroke, V4 90°, 998cm³

Gearbox
6 speed, straight cut gears

Maximum Power
235 bhp at 16,000 rpm
at the crankshaft.

Suspension
46 mm pressurized RVP2530
upside-down Öhlins fork

Brakes
Front: Brembo radial P4X30-34
Rear: Brembo radial P2X34

Weight
168kg

YAMAHA

Yamaha has been present on the FIM Superbike World Championship grid since the series began in 1988. They rank fourth in the all-time list for race wins behind Ducati, Kawasaki and Honda despite having started fewer races.

The YZF R1 engine is a four-cylinder but is unique in that it boasts a crossplane crankshaft, meaning the pistons inside the engine fire in an unconventional order. The result is a very distinct sound which means the Yamaha can be recognised audibly long before it is seen.

*From the street to the track: **YAMAHA YZF R1***

Yamaha bikes & teams   *30 Bikes, 13 Teams*

Pata Yamaha WorldSBK Team
GRT Yamaha WorldSBK
Ten Kate Racing - Yamaha

Team Toth
MS Racing
Kallio Racing
GMT94 Yamaha
BARDAHL Evan Bros. WorldSSP Team

Team MHP Racing-Patrick Pons
BCD Yamaha MS Racing
Terra e Moto
Team Trasimeno Yamaha
Semakin Di Depan Biblion Motoxracing

The idea of the crossplane is that inertia torque is reduced, allowing for a smoother power delivery for the rider.

Yamaha were back to winning ways in 2018 thanks to the efforts of Michael van der Mark and Alex Lowes. As the grid formed at Phillip Island at the start of the 2019 WorldSBK season, there was a real sense of optimism for the Japanese manufacturer as Sandro Cortese and Marco Melandri joined the fray with the factory-supported GRT outfit. Loris Baz and an all-new Ten Kate Racing / Yamaha partnership made it five Yamaha machines competing full-time from the Spanish Round at Jerez onwards.

An all-new YZF R1 will be launched ahead of the 2020 WorldSBK season, making Yamaha the dark horse for the season ahead, for which the factory has indicated continued support for their satellite teams.

With race wins in WorldSSP and WorldSSP300, Yamaha are one of the most successful manufacturers within the paddock competing across all three racing classes.

YAMAHA YZF R1

Fuel tank capacity
24 litres

Chassis
Cast aluminium

ENGINE

Type
998cc Liquid-cooled, 4-stroke, DOHC, forward-inclined parallel 4-cylinder, 4-valves

Gearbox
Constant Mesh, 6-Speed

Maximum Power
+220 hp

Suspension
Öhlins

Brakes
Brembo

Weight
168 kg

BMW

The BMW S 1000 RR was introduced purely to race in the FIM Superbike World Championship and has gone on to become one of the most commercially successful bikes on the road.

No stranger to winning races in WorldSBK, with Marco Melandri and Chaz Davies notching up no fewer than 12 victories between them across the 2012 and 2013 seasons, the Munich-based German manufacturer was back as a full factory squad in 2019 with Tom Sykes and Markus Reiterberger.

*From the street to the track: **BMW S 1000 RR***

BMW bikes & team *2 Bikes, 1 Team*

BMW Motorrad WorldSBK Team

The all-new BMW S 1000 RR launched for the 2019 WorldSBK season was lighter than its predecessor and took on ShiftCam technology in a bid to deepen torque in addition to increasing horsepower.

The all-new project impressed many with their meteoric return to the podium after just seven rounds, Tom Sykes taking second position at Misano. A historic pole position for Sykes at Donington Park followed by several more podium finishes saw Sykes end his first BMW season in well inside the top ten overall. On the other side of the garage, Reiterberger showed flashes of speed, a brace of top sixes at Assen being his season highlight. When the German was out ill, he was replaced at Donington Park by the impressive British rider Peter Hickman, who made a brief return to WorldSBK.

With riders Tom Sykes (who will remain with the squad), and Eugene Laverty confirmed for 2020, the BMW S 1000 RR, powered by an inline 4-cylinder engine, could be a title contender.

BMW S 1000 RR

Fuel tank capacity
23 litres

Chassis
Standard
BMW S 1000 RR

ENGINE

Type
four-cylinder four-stroke
in-line engine. BMW Shiftcam technology

Gearbox
Six speed

Maximum Power
+220 hp

Suspension
Öhlins

Brakes
Nissin

Weight
168 kg

HONDA

Honda won the first two FIM Superbike World Championship titles thanks to the efforts of American Fred Merkel, who took back-to-back titles for Rumi Honda in 1988 and 1989.

Back then it was the mighty RC30 750cc machine that took the spoils, whereas on today's grid Honda campaign the CBR1000RR 'Fireblade' SP2.

Present in the Championship since the very beginning, Honda take WorldSBK very seriously and in addition to the titles won by Merkel have added four more over the years thanks to John Kocinski (1997), Colin Edwards

*From the street to the track: **HONDA CBR1000RR***

Honda bikes & teams *10 Bikes, 6 Teams*

Moriwaki Althea Honda Team
Althea mie Racing Team

CIA Landlord Insurance Honda
MPM WILSport Racedays
GEMAR - Ciociaria Corse
WorldSSP Team

TGP Racing

(2000 and 2002) and James Toseland (2007).

A new partnership between Althea Racing and Moriwaki meant both parties were honoured to be running Honda's 2019 WorldSBK efforts with Leon Camier, Ryuichi Kiyonari and Alessandro Delbianco at the helm.

The road-going version of the CBR1000RR is best known for its agility and smooth engine characteristics and is an easy bike to ride quickly. In race mode, Honda's WorldSBK machine is unlike most bikes on the grid… the Fireblade uses the Nissin braking system.

After a year of data collection and work behind the scenes in Japan, HRC will launch an all-new bike to challenge in World Superbike in 2020.

Honda contested the FIM Supersport World Championship and FIM Supersport 300 World Championship in addition to WorldSBK in 2019.

HONDA CBR1000RR

Fuel tank capacity
24 litres

Chassis
Aluminium

ENGINE

Type
1000cc 4 cylinder

Gearbox
Six speed

Suspension
Öhlins

Brakes
Nissin
Yutaka 335 mm x 7 mm

Weight
168 kg

MV AGUSTA

MV Agusta Reparto Corse scaled back their presence within the FIM Superbike World Championship paddock for 2019, electing to concentrate solely on World Supersport.

Their WorldSSP contender, the MV Agusta F3 675, had been a front-runner in recent years, narrowly missing out on the World Championship title on several occasions.

*From the street to the track: **MV AGUSTA F3 675***

MV Agusta bikes & team *2 Bikes, 1 Team*

MV Agusta Reparto Corse

Experience and youth, MV Agusta went with an all Italian line-up with riders Raffaele De Rosa and Federico Fuligni tasked with bringing home the results aboard the F3 675 machine.

A new rule which standardised the ECU on all Supersport machines, combined with continued development, have enabled one of the most iconic names in motorcycling to significantly close the gap to the leaders; whilst they are still seeking that elusive first World Title in the WorldSBK paddock, one gets the feeling it isn't too far away.

MV AGUSTA *F3 675*

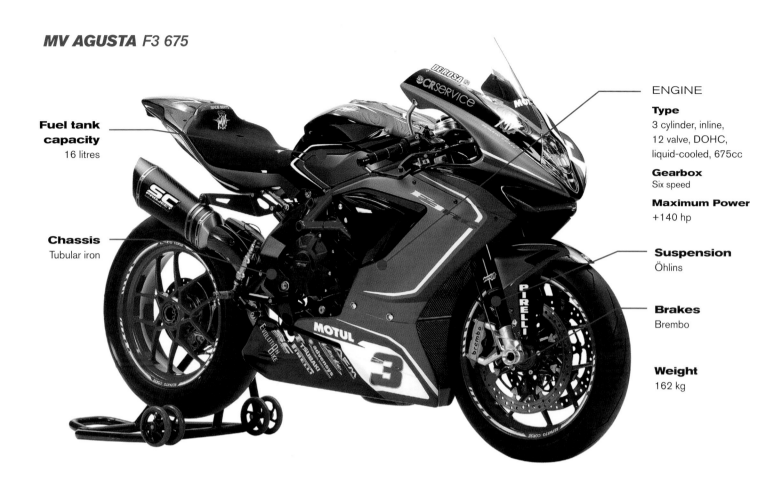

Fuel tank capacity
16 litres

Chassis
Tubular iron

ENGINE

Type
3 cylinder, inline, 12 valve, DOHC, liquid-cooled, 675cc

Gearbox
Six speed

Maximum Power
+140 hp

Suspension
Öhlins

Brakes
Brembo

Weight
162 kg

KTM

Whilst Austrian manufacturer KTM are perhaps better known for their extensive range of off-road machines - they won their first World Motocross Championship in 1974 - it was in 2003 that KTM first ventured into the world of Road Racing.

With notable Grand Prix victories in the 125cc and 250cc categories soon added to their illustrious trophy collection, KTM launched the Red Bull MotoGP Rookies Cup in 2007 and it's this support of young upcoming talent that sees them so heavily involved within the World Superbike paddock today.

*From the street to the track: **KTM RC 390 R***

KTM bikes & teams *4 Bikes, 2 Teams*

Freudenberg KTM Junior Team
Freudenberg KTM WorldSSP Team

First presented at EICMA (an Italian motorcycle exposition held every year in Milan) in 2013, the RC 390 R is an entry-level Supersport bike in its purest form. It was revised in 2017 by adding a slipper clutch, adjustable brake levers, ride-by-wire throttle, larger 320mm front brake rotor and some cosmetic and ergonomic changes.

After a strong FIM Supersport 300 World Championship debut at Jerez in 2017, where they were allowed to compete albeit without scoring points, the RC 390 R was fully homologated and able to contest the full Championship in 2018.

Dutchman Koen Meuffels gave the Austrian manufacturer a dream start to their first full season of competition, charging to victory at MotorLand Aragón in the season-opener for the KTM Fortron Team. Luca Grunwald, who won round two at the TT Circuit Assen for the Freudenberg outfit, finished fourth overall in WorldSSP300 and was a title contender heading into the final race.

In 2019 the Freudenberg KTM squad was the official WorldSSP300 entry. They entered four riders who all ran strongly throughout the year, with pole positions and a podium coming their way.

KTM *RC 390 R*

Fuel tank capacity
10 litres

Chassis
Steel trellis frame, powder-coated

ENGINE

Type
373cc 1 cylinder

Gearbox
Six speed

Maximum Power
50 hp

Suspension
WP

Brakes
Brembo

Weight
133 kg

5PIRELLI POWER

"We sell what we race, we race what we sell" has been the Pirelli motto within WorldSBK since they became the sole tyre supplier to the series in 2004.

Since then, Pirelli have combined their ethos of passion and dedication to provide all competitors with the same opportunity to compete for victory through fair and identical tyre supply for all, with forty-five individual riders standing on the podium during the last fourteen seasons in the premier class alone.

The collaboration between Pirelli and WorldSBK has always been strong, with the tyres developed and raced on track by the world's best production motorcycle racers readily available for road riders globally.

Upon completion of intense and constant development work which started in 2017 and continued throughout 2018, Pirelli introduced a new range of DIABLO™ tyres in 2019.

As in 2013 with the historic switch from 16.5-inch to 17-inch tyres, Pirelli continues to be a pioneer in development. Throughout 2018 and 2019, the Italian tyre manufacturer developed and made available several larger 200/65 rear and 125/70 front solutions for the Superbike World Championship riders. Compared to the standard sizes, the new sizes offered riders within WorldSBK greater stability, more grip thanks to the wider contact surface, and an increase in consistency in terms of performance, trajectory precision and support.

Another novelty of the 2019 season was the SCX tyre. This solution, which uses an extremely soft compound, was designed to fall between the performance of a qualifying compound and that of a soft racing tyre. It was therefore possible to use it as a pre-qualifier in order to prepare riders and bikes for the additional grip provided by the 'qualifier' tyre available for the single grid-deciding session. It also came in handy in the event of a red flag where riders could use it to finish the remaining laps of the race after a second start, being able to count on extra grip compared to their initial race choice. Finally, the SCX tyre was created as an alternative solution for the 10-lap Tissot Superpole Race on Sunday morning, giving riders and teams one more option in their strategic choices.

Understanding that today's young riders will be the future stars of WorldSBK, Pirelli continued as the sole tyre supplier to all teams and riders contesting WorldSSP, WorldSSP300, in addition to all those contesting WorldSBK.

Pirelli will continue to supply the FIM Superbike World Championship until 2023 making the contract the longest running control tyre partnership in motorcycle racing history.

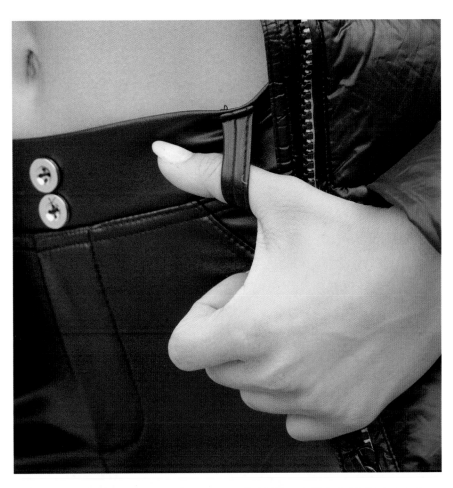

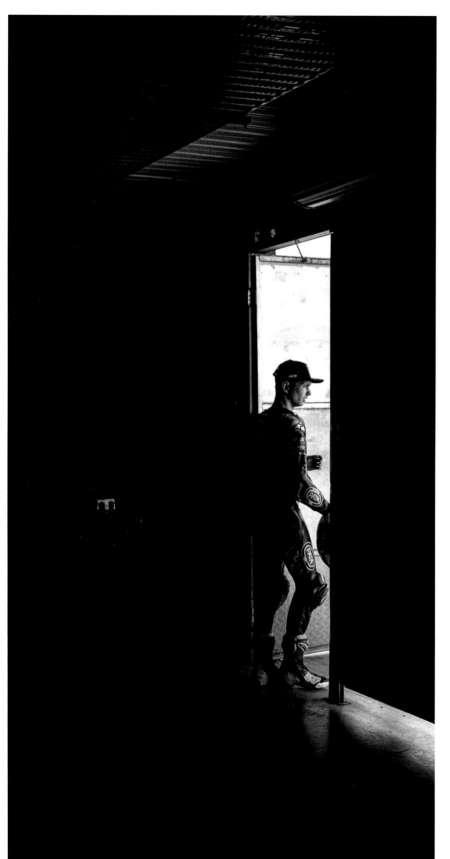

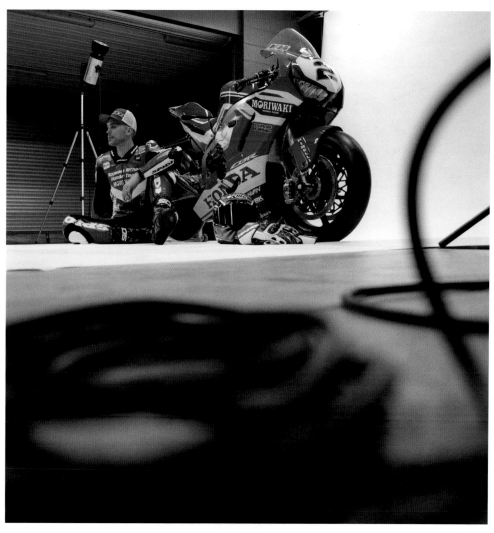

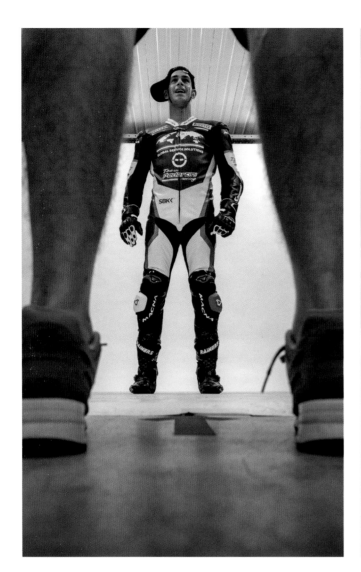

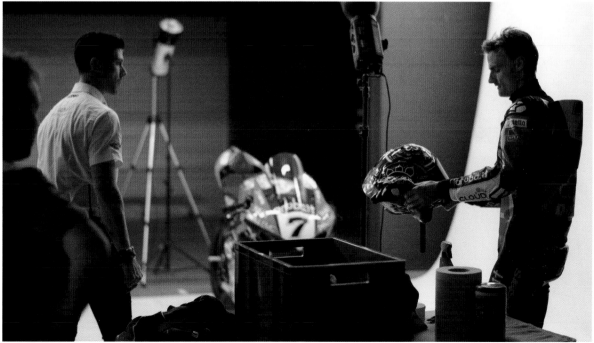

7

BEHIND THE VISORS

2019 WorldSBK RIDERS LINE UP

Jonathan Rea

Kawasaki Racing Team
WorldSBK

Leon Haslam

Kawasaki Racing Team
WorldSBK

Álvaro Bautista

Aruba.it
Racing - Ducati

Chaz Davies

Aruba.it
Racing - Ducati

Michael van der Mark

Pata Yamaha Official
WorldSBK Team

Alex Lowes

Pata Yamaha Official
WorldSBK Team

Markus Reiterberger

BMW Motorrad
WorldSBK Team

Tom Sykes

BMW Motorrad
WorldSBK Team

Michael Ruben Rinaldi

BARNI Racing Team

Replacement riders

10 **Peter Hickman** BMW Motorrad WorldSBK Team, 46 **Tommy Bridewell** Team Go Eleven, 87 **Lorenzo Zanetti** Team Go Eleven, 72 **Yuki Takahashi** Moriwaki Althea Honda Team, 13 **Takumi Takahashi** Moriwaki Althea Honda Team, 80 **Héctor Barberá** Orelac Racing Verdnatura.

Toprak Razgatlioglu

Turkish Puccetti Racing

Leon Camier

Moriwaki Althea Honda team

Ryuichi Kiyonari

Moriwaki Althea Honda team

Leandro Mercado

Orelac Racing VerdNatura

Eugene Laverty

Milwakee Aprilia

Jordi Torres

Team Pedercini Racing

Alessandro Delbianco

Althea Mie Racing Racing

Sandro Cortese

GRT Yamaha WorldSBK

Marco Melandri

GRT Yamaha WorldSBK

Loris Baz

Ten Kate Racing - Yamaha

SUPER SPORT
FIM WORLD CHAMPIONSHIP

2019 *WorldSSP* RIDERS LINE UP

36

Thomas Gradinger

Kallio Racing

84

Loris Cresson

Kallio Racing

32

Isaac Viñales

Kallio Racing

3

Raffaele De Rosa

MV AGUSTA
Reparto Corse

22

Federico Fuligni

MV AGUSTA
Reparto Corse

21

Randy Krummenacher

BARDAHL Evan Bros.
WorldSSP Team

64

Federico Caricasulo

BARDAHL Evan Bros.
WorldSSP Team

56

Peter Sebestyen

CIA Landlord
Insurance Honda

95

Jules Danilo

CIA Landlord
Insurance Honda

44

Lucas Mahias

Kawasaki
Puccetti Racing

78

Hikari Okubo

Kawasaki
Puccetti Racing

16

Jules Cluzel

GMT94 YAMAHA

178

Replacement riders

94	38	74	15	61	47
Corentin Perolari	**Hannes Soomer**	**Jaimie van Sikkelerus**	**Alfonso Coppola**	**Gabriele Ruiu**	**Rob Hartog**
GMT94 YAMAHA	MPM WILSport Racedays	MPM WILSport Racedays	GEMAR - Ciociaria Corse WorldSSP Team	GEMAR - Ciociaria Corse WorldSSP Team	Team Hartog - Against Cancer

10	30	6	86	80
Nacho Calero	**Glenn van Straalen**	**María Herrera**	**Ayrton Badovini**	**Héctor Barberá**
Orelac Racing VerdNatura	EAB Racing Team	MS Racing	Team Pedercini Racing	Team Toth by Willirace

42

Marc García

DS Junior Team

61

Yuta Okaya

DS Junior Team

84

Kim Aloisi

DS Junior Team

99

Francisco Gomez

DS Junior Team

6

Robert Schotman

Kawasaki MOTOPORT

95

Scott Deroue

Kawasaki MOTOPORT

7

Eliton Gohara Kawakami

BCD Yamaha MS Racing

25

Andy Verdoïa

BCD Yamaha MS Racing

36

Beatriz Neila

BCD Yamaha MS Racing

47

Ferran Hernandez Moyano

BCD Yamaha MS Racing

18

Manuel González

Kawasaki ParkinGO Team

27

Filippo Rovelli

Kawasaki ParkinGO Team

Replacement riders

8 **Mika Pérez** Carl Cox-RT Motorsports by SKM-Kawasaki, 9 **Steffie Naud** 2R Racing Team, 14 **Enzo de la Vega** Team MHP Racing – Patrick Pons, 17 **Koen Meuffels** Kawasaki Motoport, 26 **Joel Kelso** Nutec – RT Motorsports by SKM - Kawasaki, 51 **Dennis Koopman** MTM Racing, 57 **Livio Loi** 2R Racing Team, 94 **Eunan McGlinchey** Flembbo Leader Team ,

71	**17**	**97**	**23**	**32**	**79**	**88**
Tom Edwards	**Koen Meuffels**	**Maximilian Kappler**	**Paolo Giacomini**	**Alexandra Pelikanova**	**Tomas Alonso**	**Bruno Ieraci**
Kawasaki ParkinGO Team	Freudenberg KTM WorldSSP Team	Freudenberg KTM WorldSSP Team	Kawasaki GP Project	Kawasaki GP Project	Kawasaki GP Project	Kawasaki GP Project

13	**20**	**22**	**55**	**65**	**41**
Dino Iozzo	**Dorren Loureiro**	**Nick Kalinin**	**Galang Hendra Pratama**	**Jacopo Facco**	**Jan-Ole Jähnig**
Nutec - RT Motorsports by SKM - Kawasaki	Nutec - RT Motorsports by SKM - Kawasaki	Nutec - RT Motorsports by SKM - Kawasaki	Semakin Di Depan Biblion Motoxracing	Semakin Di Depan Biblion Motoxracing	Freudenberg KTM Junior Team

72
Victor Steeman
Freudenberg KTM
Junior Team

28
Omar Bonoli
Team Trasimeno
Yamaha

35
Finn de Bruin
Team Trasimeno
Yamaha

64
Hugo De Cancellis
Team Trasimeno
Yamaha

85
Kevin Sabatucci
Team Trasimeno
Yamaha

19
Benjamin Tomas Molina
Terra e Moto

30
Daniel Blin
Terra e Moto

11
Kevin Arduini
2R Racing Team

82
Jack Hyde
2R Racing Team

52
Oliver König
ACCR Czech Talent Team
- Willi Race

77
Vojtech Schwarz
ACCR Czech Talent Team
- Willi Race

44
Tom Bramich
Carl Cox-RT Motorsports
by SKM-Kawasaki

9
Steffie Naud
Flembbo Leader Team

63 Andrea Longo Kawasaki GP Project, **67 Taylor Fox-Moreton** ACCR Czech Talent Team – Willi Race, **68 Jarno Ioverno** Team Terra e Moto, **87 Jacob Stroud** Nutec – RT Motorsports by SKM - Kawasaki, **92 Tim Georgi** Freudenberg KTM WorldSSP Team, **52 Oliver Konig** Freudenberg KTM WorldSSP Team, **45 Muhammad Faerozi** Semakin Di Depan Biblion Motoxracing, **90 Dallas Daniels** BCD Yamaha MS Racing

14	**1**	**66**	**69**	**15**	**78**	**8**
Enzo De La Vega	**Ana Carrasco**	**Dion Otten**	**Jeffrey Buis**	**Manuel Bastianelli**	**Joseph Foray**	**Mika Pérez**
Flembbo Leader Team	Kawasaki Provec WorldSSP300	MTM Racing Team	MTM Racing Team	Prodina IRCOS Kawasaki	Prodina IRCOS Kawasaki	Scuderia Maranga Racing

21	**3**	**12**	**33**	**93**	**54**
Borja Sanchez	**Mateo Pedeneau**	**Romain Dore**	**Kyrian Hartmann**	**Adrien Quinet**	**Bahattin Sofuoglu**
Scuderia Maranga Racing	Team MHP Racing-Patrick Pons	Team MHP Racing-Patrick Pons	Team MHP Racing-Patrick Pons	TGP Racing	Turkish Puccetti Racing by TSM

03

SBK®
STATISTICS

WorldSBK Champions

YEAR	RIDER	NATIONALITY	TEAM
2019	Jonathan Rea	GBR	Kawasaki Racing Team
2018	Jonathan Rea	GBR	Kawasaki Racing Team
2017	Jonathan Rea	GBR	Kawasaki Racing Team
2016	Jonathan Rea	GBR	Kawasaki Racing Team
2015	Jonathan Rea	GBR	Kawasaki Racing Team
2014	Sylvain Guintoli	FRA	Aprilia Racing Team
2013	Tom Sykes	GBR	Kawasaki Racing Team
2012	Max Biaggi	ITA	Aprilia Racing Team
2011	Carlos Checa	ESP	Althea Racing
2010	Max Biaggi	ITA	Aprilia Alltalia Racing
2009	Ben Spies	USA	Yamaha World Superbike Team
2008	Troy Bayliss	AUS	Ducati Xerox Team
2007	James Toseland	GBR	Hanspree Ten Kate Honda
2006	Troy Bayliss	AUS	Ducati Xerox Team
2005	Troy Corser	AUS	Alstare Suzuki Corona
2004	James Toseland	GBR	Ducati FILA
2003	Neil Hodgson	GBR	Ducati FILA
2002	Colin Edwards	USA	Castrol Honda HRC
2001	Troy Bayliss	AUS	Ducati Infostrada
2000	Colin Edwards	USA	Castrol Honda HRC
1999	Carl Fogarty	GBR	Ducati Performance
1998	Carl Fogarty	GBR	Ducati Performance
1997	John Kocinski	USA	Castrol Honda HRC
1996	Troy Corser	AUS	Promotor Racing Team
1995	Carl Fogarty	GBR	Virginio Ferrari Ducati Corse
1994	Carl Fogarty	GBR	Virginio Ferrari Ducati Corse
1993	Scott Russell	USA	Team Muzzy Kawasaki
1992	Doug Polen	USA	Team Police Ducati
1991	Doug Polen	USA	Fast by Ferracci Ducati
1990	Raymond Roche	FRA	Squadra Corse Ducati Lucchinelli
1989	Fred Merkel	USA	Rumi Honda
1988	Fred Merkel	USA	Rumi Honda

WorldSSP Champions

YEAR	RIDER	NATIONALITY	TEAM
2019	Randy Krummenacher	SUI	BARDAHL Evan Bros. WorldSSP Team
2018	Sandro Cortese	GER	Kallio Racing
2017	Lucas Mahias	FRA	GRT Yamaha Official WorldSSP Team
2016	Kenan Sofuoglu	TUR	Kawasaki Puccetti Racing
2015	Kenan Sofuoglu	TUR	Kawasaki Puccetti Racing
2014	Michael van der Mark	NED	PATA Honda World Supersport
2013	Sam Lowes	GBR	Yakhnich Motorsport
2012	Kenan Sofuoglu	TUR	Kawasaki Lorenzini
2011	Chaz Davies	GBR	Yamaha ParkinGO Team
2010	Kenan Sofuoglu	TUR	Hanspree Ten Kate Honda
2009	Cal Crutchlow	GBR	Yamaha World Supersport
2008	Andrew Pitt	AUS	Hanspree Ten Kate Honda
2007	Kenan Sofuoglu	TUR	Hanspree Ten Kate Honda
2006	Sebastien Charpentier	FRA	Winston Ten Kate Honda
2005	Sebastien Charpentier	FRA	Winston Ten Kate Honda
2004	Karl Muggeridge	AUS	Ten Kate Honda
2003	Chris Vermeulen	AUS	Ten Kate Honda
2002	Fabien Foret	FRA	Ten Kate Honda
2001	Andrew Pitt	AUS	Fuchs Kawasaki
2000	Jorg Teuchert	GER	Alpha Technik Yamaha
1999	Stephane Chambon	FRA	Suzuki Alstare F.S
1998	Fabrizio Pirovano	ITA	Team Alstare Corona
1997	Paolo Casoli	ITA	Gio.Ca.Moto

WorldSSP300 Champions

YEAR	RIDER	NATIONALITY	TEAM
2019	Manuel González	ESP	Kawasaki ParkinGO Team
2018	Ana Carrasco	ESP	DS Racing Team
2017	Marc Garcia	ESP	MS Racing

Most pole positions	49	Tom Sykes	
Most race wins	83	Jonathan Rea	
Most race wins with same manufacturer	73	Jonathan Rea	Kawasaki
Most pole positions in a season	11	Ben Spies	2009
Most wins in a season	17	Doug Polen / Jonathan Rea	1991 / 2018 & 2019
Most consecutive race wins in a season	11	Jonathan Rea / Álvaro Bautista	2018 / 2019
Most race wins by a rider in their rookie season	15	Álvaro Bautista	2019
Most fastest laps in a season	14	Doug Polen / Jonathan Rea	1991 / 2017
Most laps led in a single season	287	Neil Hodgson	2003
Most crashes in a single season (since 1999)	20	Rubén Xaus	2008
Most podiums in a season	34*	Jonathan Rea	2019
Most points scored in a single season	663*	Jonathan Rea	2019

*3 races per weekend

2019 Final Championship Standings

SBK MOTUL — FIM SUPERBIKE WORLD CHAMPIONSHIP

1	Jonathan Rea	663
2	Álvaro Bautista	498
3	Alex Lowes	341
4	Michael van der Mark	327
5	Toprak Razgatlioglu	315
6	Chaz Davies	294
7	Leon Haslam	281
8	Tom Sykes	223
9	Marco Melandri	177
10	Loris Baz	138
11	Jordi Torres	135
12	Sandro Cortese	134
13	Michael Ruben Rinaldi	122
14	Markus Reiterberger	83
15	Eugene Laverty	81

Manufacturers

1	Kawasaki	673
2	Ducati	623
3	Yamaha	451
4	BMW	249
5	Honda	88

Teams

1	Kawasaki Racing Team WorldSBK	944
2	Aruba.it Racing - Ducati	792
3	PATA Yamaha WorldSBK Team	668

Independent riders

1	Toprak Razgatlioglu	315
2	Marco Melandri	177
3	Loris Baz	138

SUPERSPORT — FIM WORLD CHAMPIONSHIP

1	Randy Krummenacher	213
2	Federico Caricasulo	207
3	Jules Cluzel	200
4	Lucas Mahias	168
5	Hikari Okubo	105
6	Raffaele De Rosa	101
7	Isaac Viñales	97
8	Corentin Perolari	91
9	Thomas Gradinger	90
10	Ayrton Badovini	65
11	Peter Sebestyen	59
12	Loris Cresson	41
13	Jules Danilo	39
14	Hannes Soomer	31
15	Kyle Smith	36

Manufacturers

1	Yamaha	290
2	Kawasaki	181
3	MV Agusta	109
4	Honda	76

Teams

1	BARDAHL Evan Bros. WorldSSP Team	420
2	GMT94 Yamaha	291
3	Kawasaki Puccetti Racing	273

FIM EUROPE SUPERSPORT CUP

1	Kyle Smith	17

SUPERSPORT300 — FIM WORLD CHAMPIONSHIP

1	Manuel González	161
2	Scott Deroue	131
3	Ana Carrasco	117
4	Andy Verdoïa	97
5	Victor Steeman	69
6	Marc García	68
7	Galang Hendra Pratama	64
8	Jan-Ole Jähnig	61
9	Hugo de Cancellis	54
10	Nick Kalinin	48
11	Bruno Ieraci	46
12	Kevin Sabatucci	41
13	Koen Meuffels	36
14	Jeffrey Buis	25
15	Tom Edwards	24

Manufacturers

1	Kawasaki	216
2	Yamaha	129
3	KTM	86

Teams

1	Kawasaki ParkinGO Team	188
2	Kawasaki MOTOPORT	160
3	Freudenberg KTM Junior Team	130

SBK® thanks to

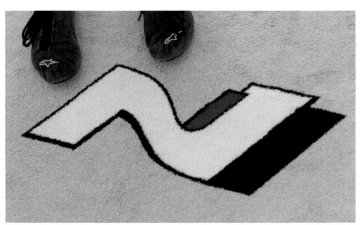

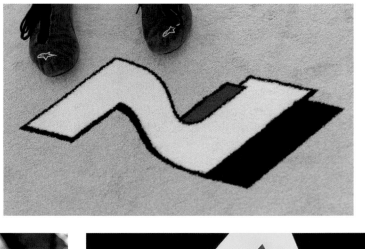

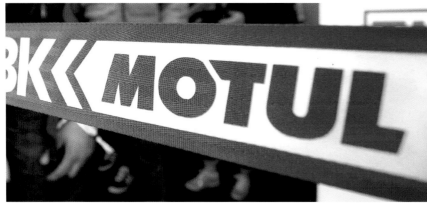

WE MAKE EXCITEMENT